THE REMNANT CHURCH

Volume One: The Who and Why

THE SUM TOTAL OF ALL THINGS

Bishop Ronald D. Roston

The Remnant Church, The Sum Total of All Things:
Volume 1 "The Who & Why"
Copyright © 2021 Ronald Roston
~ Official Release ~

Cover Design: C Marcel Wiggins

All rights reserved. No part of this publication may be reproduced, distributed or transmitted in any form or by any means, without prior written permission. Unless otherwise identified, scripture quotations are from the King James Version of the Bible.

Publisher
Dreamer Reign Media, LLC
P.O. Box 291354
Port Orange, FL 32129

www.dreamerreign.com

For Worldwide Distribution
Printed in the U.S.A.

ISBN: 9781952253041
Library of Congress Control Number: 2021952757

CONTENTS

Dedication..4

Preface..5

Chapter One: The Remnant...11

Chapter Two: Why A Remnant Church?................................75

Chapter Three: The Sum Total & The Remnant................. 137

Endnotes... 181

This book is volume 1 of a 4 volume set. The second volume contains chapters 4 - 6. The third volume contains chapters 7 - 9. The fouth volume contains all chapters (1 - 9) and additional notes and references.

DEDICATION

In addition to Jehovah, Jesus, and The Holy Spirit, I dedicate this work to the Body of Christ, my spiritual family; the Church...the living organism which the Father has chosen to be co-laborers with Jesus Christ, harbingers of the deliverance, grace, and mercy of the Ancient of Days.

I thank God for my beloved wife, LaCreece, who encouraged me to birth this body of information, and her shared concern for the saints to have access to this material. I bless the Father for giving me a "good thing" to walk with me in ministry.

I bless the Most High for the Servant Warriors with whom I share ministry: Bishop C.A. Roston; Bishop Jamar Suber; Bishop Roy Etienne Smith; Bishop Cardijn Mokube; Elder Keith Cash; Rev. Elliott Hampton, and Rev. Michael Harris. I love these brothers dearly, and appreciate the gifts and graces they contribute to the Church.

Last, but not least, I devote this project to my natural and spiritual sons and daughters worldwide. My hope and prayer is that this material will help them mature into the children of God they are predestined to become by His grace.

I am grateful that Jehovah commissioned me to "do the work."

PREFACE

Having been led by the Spirit of God, and in obedience to Him, I pen these words and thoughts. I merely lend myself as a vessel of expression for Him to use. I yield my gifts, talents, and graces to Him to use (as He will) to accomplish His purposes in the earth. This literary work has nothing to do with my abilities, but everything to do with His direction and inspiration upon my thinking. It is my response to His impression on some critical issues we must examine, as this earth and time heads for a collision with God and eternity.

There appears to be a condition in the Church which is causing a misrepresentation among unbelievers, as to just who the Body of Christ is. There are some general misconceptions as to the identity of "the called out one," what they look like, how they function, and just what they do and do not possess. It can also be said that these same types of issues and concerns can be found within the Body of Christ, itself. There is a need for clarity because of these misnomers, and the resulting effect they have on the lives of society. Humanity's response, or lack of response, to the Master's invitation to come out from among them and be ye separate, makes it necessary to begin to distinguish what is and what is not Christianity. This situation drives us to examine Christianity, as it lines up to how God has called the Church to function, and address what God calls the Church to look like.

The very nature of this type of examination will surely cause eyebrows to raise and cries of, "how dare you stand in judgment of the Body of Christ" being heard from every corner of Christendom. "Who gives you the right" will ooze off of the lips of saints and sinners alike, as this work attempts to draw a line in the sand. As we set up examination criteria as a means of determining if the Church is in fact living up to God's expectations of her, there will be criticism from both far and wide. I can remember my father teaching me a lesson, when I was newly saved. He said, "If you are walking down the street and you see a man run out of the bank with a stocking cap covering his face, a gun in his hand, and a sack of money thrown over his back, you do not have to make a judgment that he is a bank robber. The facts that are blaring in your face clearly tell you that he is a bank robber.

There are times when we are confronted with "in your face" facts that plainly confirm what you believe to be true. As such, you are not judging when you form your opinion; you are merely standing in agreement to what the facts validate as truth. Such is the case as we begin this examination as to where the Church presently stands in terms of its current behavior, and how it correlates to how God says the Church should be functioning here at the end of time. Yet, we dare ask the question, "Is it not the responsibility of the senior members of this organism, this live, functioning body of believers, to take an inventory to determine if the Church is on point?" Is she on schedule? Is she on task? Is she living up to God's mandate for us to be an extension of the ministry of Jesus Christ in the earth? Are we fulfilling our responsibility to replicate the actions of the author and finisher of our faith? Is our face and actions set to the task of destroying the works of the devil, and reconciling the world unto God? Do we have the propagation of the advancement of the principles of the Kingdom of God in the earth, as our central motivation and number one priority? Are we determined to keep the unity of the Spirit in the bond of peace? Is the love of God the driving force behind all that we do? Or do we come up lacking in these areas? Is the Body "missing the mark" when it comes to these things? These are questions we have to answer affirmatively if we are to function in our destiny and purpose, as we operate at the end of time. If the Church is not meeting these benchmarks, what needs to be done to insure that the Body does what's necessary to come up to speed?

If it is not the Body of Christ that asks these soulsearching questions, if it is not the saints of the Lord God Jehovah, creator of heaven and earth, who push the envelope to determine these critically needed answers in the time of the global crisis in which the world finds itself, then who will sincerely take on this task? If not us who; if not now, when? It is the duty of those who claim relationship to the Ancient of Days, to take an honest inventory of just how successful the "ecclesia" is doing in operating in her God appointed capacity. Do we truly exist to reconcile the world unto Jehovah, wage war against the kingdom of darkness, and function as duly authorized designated representatives and delegated authorities of Christ? We must take a painstaking evaluation of the Church, her motives and objectives, if we are to truthfully answer these questions. They must be answered without trying to safeguard our reputation or hide any apparent flaws, if we are ever to be the end time body of believers that actually serves as an extension of the ministry of Christ in the earth.

As this work begins to examine those types of questions, it is not the author's intention to make a judgment of the Church.

Conversely, it is our intention to stimulate the Body to critically examine our condition, as an attempt to foster a catalyst for positive change. Our desire is to motivate those who seek to emerge out of the mundane rote worship and existence that has invaded Christendom, to implement the changes necessary to catapult the Church to a state of functionality, that separates her from the "Church as usual" body and transforms her into "the remnant Church."

Know that you are loved, empowered and ordained; as the family of God, we are predestined to become "THE REMNANT CHURCH"

I love you in Jesus' name!

Your brother in arms,

Apostle Ronald D. Roston, D. Min. - ROMI

International Presiding Bishop & General Overseer

Restoration Oasis Ministries International

Senior Pastor - Times of Refreshing Ministries

Founder/Chief Facilitator

Apostolic Kingdom Covenant Ministries / AKC Ministries

"Even so then at this present time also there is a remnant according to the election of grace. And if by grace, then is it no more of works: otherwise grace is no more grace. But if it be of works, then is it no more grace: otherwise work is no more work."
Romans 11:5-6

Chapter One
The Remnant

"Remnant: the part of something that is left when other parts are gone." The definition for this word is so simplistic, yet it represents an extremely complex and detailed idea that involves the notion of something smaller being used to accomplish that which the larger part failed to accomplish. The idea that something which is void of its other parts, parts which appeared to be necessary, is still able to function in the purpose and role for which it was created, and intended to be used. The remnant is a mystery that causes us to wonder how that which remains still has the power and capacity to fulfill the mission that was assigned to the whole—the remnant!

The remnant is a concept that really has not received a lot of attention from the Church until recently. However, it seems to be circulating in the group of saints with whom I am associated and gaining increasing popularity. It is a concept I have been espousing since 2011. Although this conversation may be considered to be in its infancy, it is yet a concept that is crucial to our understanding just how God will deal with humanity, here at the end of time. This idea is so central to Christianity, that the theme is interwoven into the entire Bible story in one form or another.

As we examine the lineage of the children of Adam and Eve. It can be found in the account of Noah and the flood. Look again and you will see it in the call of faithful Abram. Obviously, we see it in the narrative of Isaac and Ishmael. How could we miss it as we study the rift between Jacob and Esau? How evident it is when viewing the separation of Joseph from his brothers? What about the group of African Edenic Hebrews that left Egypt in the "Exodus," and the separation God allowed as He split the camp with venomous vipers? It is easy to note as we see the descendants of Abraham split into the two kingdoms of Israel and Judah.

As we become aware of the Jews who remained faithful to Jehovah as their kings exposed them to pagan worship and deities, and while in exile remained faithful; we find "the remnant."

The concept is as prevalent in the New Testament as it is in the Old Testament. Although the physical word may not be present in a lot of the Biblical text, to try to comprehend God's

CHAPTER ONE: THE REMNANT

relationship with man, without giving credence to this notion, would be a mistake of grave proportions. The impact of God dealing with some things or persons that have survived destruction or a separation of some sort, tells the story of many of the Bible's central characters. There has always been a remainder or residue from a particular group after the majority of that group has been removed in one way or another. This constitutes a remnant. Even as we rehearse the familiar concept of "the rapture" or "the catching away," however you choose to term it; the notion of a remnant is completely intertwined in that discussion.

"For we shall not all sleep, but we shall be changed in a moment, in the twinkling of an eye. And those of us who do remain (the remnant) shall be caught up to meet him in the air..."

The Holy Spirit speaks a singular message to the Body of Christ; He speaks it plainly, succinctly, and repeatedly. Those who have an ear to hear, listen to what the Spirit of God is speaking to the Church. Understand what the remnant represents and why it is critical to end times ministry and the role of the Church at the end of the age. As we witness an unprecedented "spirit of compromise" in the Church, as we witness the erosion of some central core values and beliefs among believers, there is a remnant being formed. As the Church rocks and reels from scandal after scandal, and previously solid progenitors of "the faith" begin to waiver on fundamental issues, a remnant is being formed. As the government seeks to impose its sanctions on freedom of speech over the electronic airways, on TV, and radio, and remove basic rights of the Church to use the name of Jesus, a remnant is being formed.

As groups within the Body of Christ justify behavior and practices that are in direct contradiction to the tenets of the faith that were passed onto us by the patriarchs and apostolic fathers of this great Christianity, a remnant is being formed! Think about it, it was the remnant of Adam's sons that God chose to deal with—Seth. Out of all the other sons he had, the Bible only records Seth and his descendants as having any consequential impact upon the future of mankind. In fact, it was only after Seth grew up and had a son named Enosh/Enos that people first began to worship Yahweh by name. The King James Bible refers to it like this,

> *The Holy Spirit speaks a singular message to the Body of Christ; He speaks it plainly, succinctly, and repeatedly. Those who have an ear to hear, listen to what the Spirit of God is speaking to the Church.*

"And to Seth, to him also there was born a son; and he called his name Enos: then began men to call upon the name of the Lord." Genesis 4:26

It was through the lineage of Seth that Lamech, the father of Noah, was born. Imagine the whole of humanity so continually inclining their thoughts toward evil that they were willing to enter into negotiations with the fallen angels.

"And it came to pass, when men began to multiply on the face of the earth, and daughters were born unto them, That the sons of God saw the daughters of men

CHAPTER ONE: THE REMNANT

that they were fair; and they took them wives of all they chose." Genesis 6:1-2

They were arranging for these beings, which had lost their heavenly estate, to marry the daughters of men. This foul union produced the race of giants. These creatures, upon their death, released what we know as "familiar spirits" into the earth. God was so sorry that He even created mankind; He chose to destroy the entire world. He only chose a remnant of humanity to experience His mercy and grace: Noah, his wife Mrs. Noah, Noah's sons: Shem, Ham, and Japheth, and their wives. The entire known world was decimated because of their unbelief, the entire creation was destroyed; only eight people were left over; a remnant!

"And all flesh died that moved upon the earth, both of fowl, and of cattle, and of beast, and of every creeping thing that creepeth upon the earth, and every man: All in whose nostrils was the breath of life, of all that was in the land, died. And every living substance was destroyed upon the face of the ground, both man, and cattle, and the creeping things, and the fowl of the heaven; and they were destroyed from the earth: and Noah only remained alive, and they that were with him in the ark." Genesis 7:21-23

Japheth and Ham both left the place that represented the second cradle of civilization, the place where God had decided to reestablish His creation. Japheth went north, (his sons and their families) Tarshish (Italy), Javan, Tiras, Gomer (Turkey, Russia, Ukraine, Bulgaria), Ashkenaz, Lud, Meshech, Dodanim (Lebanon), Tubal, Togarman, Hamath (Syria), Greece, Cyprus, Romania and settled what would ultimately become known as Europe. Ham moved south, (his sons and their families) Put, Lehabim, Lubim, Mizraim (Egypt), Cush (Sudan), Seba (Ethiopia), Sheba, Dedan, (Saudi Arabia), Ophir, Pathrusim, Havilah (Saudi Arabia), Raamah, Libya, Malta, Tunisia, Algeria and settled what would ultimately become known as (Africa). Only Shem, his sons and their families, rested in the land where the Ark settled. (Saudi Arabia, Jordan, Iran, Iraq, Pakistan, Afghanistan, India). Not only did he settle what was to become known as the Holy Land, but he also became the progenitor of the line that would produce Messiah Jesus; Jesus Ha' Mashiach. God used what was left over, He used what remained, Shem, to fulfill the promise He had made in the Garden of Eden. In Eden, the Creator spoke of there being enmity, hostility, mutual hatred, antagonism, animosity, rivalry between the offspring of the devil and the offspring of the woman. That hostility would bruise the heel of the Messiah, but it would crush the head of the devil.

"And I will put enmity between thee and the woman, and between thy seed and her seed;" Genesis 3:15

Could God have possibly known what would happen between the fallen angels and the daughters of men, in Noah's day? Of course He did; He knows the end from the beginning. Could He have known about the offspring that would be created as the fallen angels saw the daughters of men, that they were pleasant, and took as they would for wives? Did He have foreknowledge of the demons and familiar spirits which were to be released on mankind and how they would war for the souls of men? Of course He

CHAPTER ONE: THE REMNANT

did. This is why He prophesied in the Garden of Eden about the warfare that would take place between these groups.

"And I will put enmity between thee and the woman, and between thy seed and her seed; and it shall bruise thy head, and thou shalt bruise his heel."
Genesis 3:15

There is nothing that is a surprise to God. There is no way for us to fool Him; yet He still allows us to have a "free will" and exercise the privilege of choice He bequeaths upon us as a gracious father bestows gifts upon his children. Abram was what was left over after the languages were confused at Babel. Another remnant, he now stood as the only one in the whole earth having access to the Lord God Jehovah; Yahweh.

"Go to, let us go down, and there confound their language, that they may not understand one another's speech. So the Lord scattered them abroad from thence upon the face of all the earth: and they left off to build the city. Therefore is the name of it called Babel; because the Lord did there confound the language of all the earth: and from thence did the Lord scatter them abroad ..." Genesis 11:7-9

"Now the Lord had said unto Abram, Get thee out of thy country, and from thy kindred, and from thy father's house, unto a land that I will show thee:"
Genesis 12:1

He arose out of the confusion, to now stand as the only man having total exclusivity to a Heavenly Father, that had once been available to all mankind. Out of the midst of a creation of whom ALL had access to God, only he and his descendants alone, could now claim to have covenant relationship with the Ancient of Days. If anyone else wanted to have relationship with Jehovah, they

> *"There is nothing that is a surprise to God. There is no way for us to fool Him; yet He still allows us to have a "free will" and exercise the privilege of choice..."*

had to become a part of Abraham's people in order to worship the God who Abraham worshipped. As God transitioned from absolute inclusivity, He transformed Himself to being exclusively the God of the Hebrews. Only Abraham, Isaac, and Jacob could now claim to be the recipients of having communion with the God of creation. If anyone else wanted to have communion with God, they had to be in covenant relationship with Abraham and his descendants, that was the exception they had to fulfill. It was only Abraham's descendants, and those who would become proselytes of what would come to be known as Judaism, who could hope to benefit from the grace and mercy God was extending from heaven to earth. They were the remnant.

"And I will make of thee a great nation, and I will bless thee, and make thy name great; and thou shalt be a blessing: And I will bless them that bless thee, and curse him that curseth thee: and in thee shall all families of the earth be blessed." Genesis 12:2

Then, there is David, the youngest of Jesse's sons. The whole group of Jesse's male offspring was presented before Samuel the prophet. Samuel was tasked to choose the Lord's anointed servant to replace Saul as the king of Israel.

I Samuel 16:1-13. The entire collection of Jesse's sons passed by the eye of the prophet, yet the future king was not in their midst. So, the questions were asked, "What's left over, what remains, who is the remnant that I have not yet seen?" [Surely God did not lie when He told me that I would find the chosen king of Israel among your sons, Jesse. Where is the balance of your sons, where is the one that yet remains to be seen? Bring me the remnant Jesse, so God's Word and promise can come to fruition.]

There is a Church rising out of the Church, one Church that has not yet been seen. There is a body of believers so dedicated to the doctrine passed on to us by the apostolic fathers of the 1st century Church, that they would rather stay hidden, and be ridiculed for their non-conformity. They refuse to buy into the ethical and moral compromise the Church has allowed to seep within her walls. They are a group that yet remains to be seen and identified as progenitors of the Christian faith. They are more concerned with equipping the saints to endure to the end, rather than entertaining them to make them think they have a "religion they can feel." This remnant is not concerned with title and position, but rather is bound to the concept of "functionality" as the gauge of one's position in Christ. They have been blessed with a deposit of righteousness and steadfastness that will make Israel jealous of the zeal that they possess for the God of the Hebrews. God is waiting to reveal this remnant to the nations.

Invariably, as we begin a discussion about the concept of the remnant, we must first acknowledge that in order for the remnant to exist, there must first be a main body of people or things out of which this remnant has been extracted. That being said, it is impossible to talk about the remnant of the Church or the remnant of Israel without first acknowledging the veracity or authenticity of those two bodies. A remnant is usually a small part, member, or trace remaining, a small surviving group—often used in plural, an unsold or unused end of piece goods, still remaining. The Middle English, contraction of remenant is from Anglo-French remanant, which is from the present participle of remainder.

==Remainder means to remain: to be a part not destroyed, taken, or used up; to be something yet to be shown, done, or treated; to stay in the same place or with the same person or group; especially to stay behind, to continue unchanged.==

    We are speaking of a group of people who possess the full virtues and attributes of the original group. They have embraced the purpose for which the original group even had existence. Although a smaller group numerically, it is a group that is as large in vision and purpose as the original one. The larger group is the one that has had their vision and purpose changed—compromised. This smaller group, this remnant, remains steadfast, unmovable, always abounding in the work of the Lord, with the knowledge that their labor of love is not in vain. This remnant is sold out to the same type of sacrificial love that Messiah Jesus had as He voluntarily left His home in glory, allowed Himself to be fashioned in the image of human man, took upon Himself the role of a servant, and yielded to the cruel death of the cross.

This group continues to operate in the purpose for which it was created. It continues to demonstrate the trait that identifies it as being disciples of the Christ. "Sacrificial love" permeates everything the remnant does. It is the driving motivation that permits them to endure the disassociation from the larger group. It is the bedrock upon which their faith is built, and the substance that sustains them as they refuse to change from operating in the foundational principles upon which this great Church was built. It is the anchor that keeps the remnant within the veil as they continue unseen, unchanged and faithful to the dictates of the Father.

It is from the latter definitions that we would like to center our discussion of the concept of "The Remnant Church." We contend that the remnant is something that is yet to be shown or done. It is a manifestation of the Church that has stayed behind, despite the contemporary shifts in our presentation of Christianity, to exist as the Church that "continues" unchanged. As one of my great contemporaries, Bishop Otis L. Carswell states, "The old Church is dying and must do so. The true Church of our Lord and Savior Jesus Christ is EMERGING out of that old Church; that old system of doing things." The Church triumphant is that Remnant Church; the Church that has stayed in place and continued in the Apostle's doctrine as recorded in Acts 2:42,

"And they continued steadfastly in the apostles' doctrine and fellowship, and in breaking of bread and in prayers."

It is a small part or body of believers. It is the unused part that has not been destroyed by the contemporary shifts, which have been responsible for causing the Church to look like the world. Those shifts which have made it hard to distinguish whether you are listening to gospel music or the latest releases from the world of hip hop, rhythm and blues, and jazz. These attempts to make the Church "palatable" and appealing to the world have made it hard to recognize if you are listening to a presentation of the gospel message, or to a reiteration of the latest world news or an emotional presentation of social doctrines. The remnant is that "trace" which remains committed to look and act like the original body from which it was extracted; not the current Church, but the original Church. It is the sign or evidence of the past state in which the Church operated, known as holiness. It is a minute and sometimes barely detectable amount or indication of the place of power in which the Church was initially birthed. The remnant is that tiny speck of power that has not been compromised by the wiles of the enemy, as he attempts to make the testimony of the saints null and void. This group refuses to be invalidated and made of non-effect, because of her allowance of the operating principles of this world to influence her look and sound. She remains true to the stature from which she was formed, and will not allow her mold to be broken. Every fiber of her being smells with the sweet aroma of the presence of the Spirit of God; that

> *"The remnant is that tiny speck of power that has not been compromised by the wiles of the enemy, as he attempts to make the testimony of the saints null and void."*

same presence that was so obvious on the Day of Pentecost.

The concept of a remnant deals with the idea of a "balance" or something left over. It endorses the idea of a "remainder" or put another way, an amount in excess; especially on the credit side of an account. "Leftovers," as it were, refer to something that remains unused or unconsumed; especially leftover food served at a later meal. That's what the remnant is something that remains unused or unconsumed by the current trends which are causing the Church to be "blended" into the world. Those practices which make Christianity an item that easily fits into the category of being a "cross-over" commodity, mandates that a balance of uncompromised leftovers exist in order to perpetuate the true mission of the Church...to come out from among them and be ye separated, says the Lord of Hosts. The remnant has to be that unconsumed leftover food that can be used to satisfy the hunger of a dying, emaciated world as it cries out, "What must I do to be saved?" There has to be a balance of something left over, that truly represents the flavor and consistency of the original fodder, which was left in place to satisfy the hunger of a sin-sick world.

The main priority in which the Church was established centered on reconciling the creation back to the Father, and ministering deliverance from the grips of the evil one. Both of these are representative of what Jesus was charged to do. This is what He did as He left eternity and made His incursion into our dwelling sphere known as time.

"For this purpose the Son of God was manifested, that He might destroy the works of the devil." I John. 3:8b.

What are "the works of the enemy?" In the onslaught that happened in the Garden of Eden, the enemy was able to separate the creation from the Creator. Man was created in perfect harmony with God. They were united by the Spirit of God, which Jehovah breathed into His creation, a creation crafted from the dirt of the earth. Man was perfect and had no knowledge of evil. When Adam and Eve partook of the fruit, they were exposed to the knowledge of good and evil. Evil is disobedience to the Word, or law, of God. This knowledge contaminated their Spirit, and caused it to be disconnected from the Spirit of God. Man's spirit became dead, hence the condition known as "spiritual death" came into the world. Consequently, the need arose for man to be "born-again;" man needed a spiritual rebirth.

The work that the enemy of our soul was able to accomplish was to change the nature, or spirit, of man from being holy and perfect. He performed a "spiritual assassination," which resulted in the admittance of mental & physical sickness, and spiritual & physical death into this sphere known as time on this place known as earth. Jesus came to undo all that satan had accomplished, and has commissioned His Church to do the same. This mandate to destroy the works of the enemy serves as the reason the Church was birthed, and how she has been instructed to operate until Jesus returns to rapture her. Where is the remnant? Where are those who will season the world with the flavor of God? Where are the people that will stand in the gap to preserve the creation? Where are those who will replicate the compassion the Father had for His deceived creation? For God so loved the world that He gave. He gave the best that Heaven had to offer. He gave Himself. He

CHAPTER ONE: THE REMNANT

allowed His creative component known as "The Word" to fulfill prophecy, manifest out of eternity and be housed in human flesh; live a sinless life; die a substitutionary death, and be resurrected from the dead. He did all of this in order to redeem His creation from the sentence of death imposed upon them as a result of "the fall."

Jehovah could have condemned the creation because of their disobedience, destroyed them, and started all over again from the beginning, but He didn't. Instead, He made the ultimate sacrifice; He allowed Himself to carry the "sin of the world" in a human body of flesh. He separated Himself, and turned His back on that sin ladened God-man, known as Jesus of Nazareth. He Himself paid the penalty for the crime that was committed in the Garden. His act of kindness provided a pardon for mankind and subsequent access to God again, by giving the creation the free gift of eternal life. Who wouldn't serve a God like our God?

The remnant doesn't blend into the look and sound of the presentation of Christianity that is trying to seduce the world into salvation by sending that oh so dangerous message, "See, we are just like you." The remnant is not saying, "The only difference between us is that we have accepted Jesus Christ as our personal Savior." Our message is uncompromised, and parallels the original Good News that was presented, with repentance as the requisite; we are labeled as "odds and ends." The remnant is seen as miscellaneous articles and small matters to be attended to. We don't really count; we are remnants. The remnant is not a part of the larger whole; it is even considered to be cultish, because it doesn't agree or buy into the popular notion of Christianity currently being espoused by men and women who command the attention of a large national and international audience.

I would much rather be a remnant, than to be a part of a large body of believers who are missing the purposes of God, and walking in a manner that is not becoming that of being a royal priesthood and a holy nation. I would much rather be a miscellaneous article that is "peculiar" and distinguished, than an unrecognizable part of a larger group that is missing the mark originally intended for the ecclesia. Call me crazy, but I would much rather be a leftover than something that is consumed and all used up. The remnant can ill-afford to function in a capacity that is not in alignment with the original purpose of the initial Church.

There is an inherent danger in not functioning in accordance to one's purpose. One of the most prolific Bible teachers of our time, Dr. Myles Monroe, said it this way, *"If something is not functioning according to its purpose, then abuse is inevitable."* Since God is ultimately in control of everything, and there is nothing that is a surprise to Him, once He has decided that it is time for the remnant to emerge, it must function in accordance to the purpose that the Father has assigned to it. If the stage has been set for the present-day conformist, deceived, compromised Church to move aside in deference to the remnant, then the remnant must operate in its own purpose. Otherwise, the remnant will be confused as being the current conformist-Church. It will not be recognized as different from it.

The danger in operating outside of purpose is that something cannot fulfill the destiny for which it was created. If the remnant fails to fulfill its purpose, it will not be able to accomplish the things that God has decreed it to do here at the end of the age. Therefore, not walking in purpose has the potential of elongating the time table for the fulfillment of all things purposed by the Ancient of Days. In addition to sending a confusing message to the unsaved, by not operating according to God's purpose for it, the remnant also has the potential to cripple Christians who are discontent with the conformist, deceived, compromised Church, and are looking for a God-given alternative. Unless the remnant is operating in its God-given purpose, it will not be the agent of continuity, reflecting the exousia (authority) and dunamis (ability) of the 1st century Church, the Church that adhered to the apostle's doctrine. This doctrine that was passed on to the apostles by the Christ of God Himself.

The "remnant" has been challenged to abide: to wait for the coming change. She is commanded to await the arrival of the metamorphosis that will transform her into the Church triumphant: the reflection of the New Testament Church that was in the earth and "turned the world upside down." Thus, the remnant must endure without yielding. She must endure the criticism and ridicule that labels her as "holy rollers" who are too stiff to conform to the compromising rendition of Christianity prevalent here at the end of the age.

The remnant must remain steadfast, unmovable, holding fast to the profession of her faith and to the principles that were handed down to her by the Church fathers, and the apostles who crafted the framework, built upon the foundation laid by Christ. She cannot yield to the temptation to give in to the pressure, lower the standard of holiness, and adorn the garments of carnality and sensuality. She has been commissioned to abide, to remain anchored in the hope of her expectation that God has called her to a position of righteousness that is realistic and attainable. The remnant must withstand the enticement to water down the Gospel of the Lord in an attempt to coerce the unbelieving world to accept the concept of a loving God that will not chastise His creation. She must bear patiently, the weight of the mantle that has been placed on her. She must tolerate, and accept without objection, the hatred the world has for her, because of her stance for righteousness and her adherence to the doctrine that was handed down to her by the 1st century apostles and prophets.

The remnant must remain steadfast in her determination to replicate the ministry of Jesus Christ in the earth. As she recognizes that her objective is to be a mirror image of the ministry of reconciliation provided by Jesus, it will serve as the mortar that cements her in the role God has predestined her to play in end-times ministry. She must buy into the fact that the Church is fixed in a state of transition, as she blossoms into the Church that forcefully shakes the kingdom of darkness in this present age.

The Church is not standing still; she is in constant motion. She is on a journey that will return her to her original state of power. Though it might seem that she is afflicted and stagnant, she is constantly being restored and healed. She is headed back to her position of prominence in the affairs of this world. Change is an absolute truth that cannot be ignored. The fact of the matter is that the Ancient of Days is returning the Church back to her original state of power. The fire and zeal that were present in the 1st century Church, as she turned the world upside down with the presentation of the Gospel message, accompanied by signs and wonders, shall once again be the evidence by which the true Body of Christ in the earth is identified.

When the Roman government made Christianity the official religion of the Roman Empire, it snatched the leadership of the Church out of the hands of the Jewish apostles, and launched the Church into a decline. We refer to this as the dark ages of the Church; her spiritual vitality began to decline. She remained in decline until the Protestant Reformation. It was at this time that God began to restore moves of His Spirit back into the Church. This restoration will continue until the full-blown emergence of the remnant. This emergence will be the time that the Church has returned to the place of power and effectiveness that was so noticeable after the Day of Pentecost.

The remnant must continue in this place of transition as she sojourns as strangers and pilgrims in this world. She cannot forego the pruning and perfecting that God has determined as necessary to remove the dross, and allow the pure gold to rise to the top. She does this with the knowledge that her citizenship is not of this world, but has foundation in the realm of eternity, and in fact this realm is the place to which her spiritual existence will be physically translated. Although the Church operates in the sphere of time and the limitation it imposes, her existence in the sphere of eternity provides the basis for the supernatural power she possesses, and her ability to perform the miraculous. If her citizenship and power were grounded in this world of time, she would not have the capacity to alter physical and mental situations—representative of healing, miracles, and deliverance.

The Church, nor the remnant, should allow the secular world to dictate how they operate, or set their guidelines and goals. Therefore, their reality should not be framed by the dictates of this world, but rather by the dictates of heaven. Their governance should come subject to the eternal standard of God, as opposed to submitting to the standards of this world. These ecclesiastical bodies must be governed by the principles of the place where their citizenship has been established: the eternal dwelling place of God, eternity. For example, if you try to run a non-profit organization by the rules that are used to run a for-profit corporation, mayhem will ensue. You cannot effectively operate an organism with mandates designed and intended for an organization from a completely different category. In order for either of those two bodies of believers to experience any modicum of success, there must be synergistic dynamics in play between the eternal Kingdom of God, the Church, and the remnant.

The remnant actually has its purpose founded upon the original purpose of the 1st century Church. The fact that the contemporary Church is conformist verifies the reality that she has not operated within the guidelines of her original purpose. Subsequently, it is the responsibility of the remnant to step up to the plate, and fulfill the original purpose for which the Church was left in the earth.

Therefore, it is safe to say that these two institutions are dependent on each other. The contemporary conformist-Church needs the remnant to exist in order for the original purpose of the Church to be actualized and fulfilled. However, the remnant has no existence without the Church being conformist, and thereby substantiating the need for a Remnant Church. Both of them are dependent upon being governed by eternal citizenship and the laws of the Kingdom of God, versus being governed by secular citizenship and the laws of this world. This earth is merely the place where they subject themselves to the laws of their place or origin and citizenship, in order to fulfill the purposes of God in allowing them to be here. They are His delegated authorities and designated representatives in the earth. They are to be fruitful, multiply, replenish the earth with their kind, subdue the earth, and have dominion over it.

There is a mind-bending fact we have to be aware of, and it poses a somewhat troublesome reality. This is the fact, "The remnant is a 'remaining' group, a part or trace of a larger portion, a number left after a subtraction, the final undivided part after division that is less than the original divisor." The remnant is not a large, ominous body, but it is the leftovers. Then, by definition the remnant is not considered to be a large, robust, ample portion, but conversely, it is usually thought to be lacking quantity and sometimes, quality. It is often categorized as not being enough to generate satisfaction. The remnant is not something that is coveted or sought after. It is not an item that is usually desired. It is not an object of obsession for those who are in search of being fully satisfied.

So, the obvious question is how can this remnant be capable of carrying out what needs to be accomplished by the end time Church? How can this body of believers, who are only a small portion of the larger body, have the strength, resources, and physical bodies to do the work of reaping the end time harvest before the second coming of Jesus Christ? These are pertinent questions which need a believable answer, if the remnant is expected to shoulder up under the heavy responsibility associated with its mandate to reap the harvest. We shall attempt to bring some clarity to these questions as we progress deeper into this discussion.

As we explore these questions and look for a viable answer, the only spiritually logical explanation we can give centers around what Jesus told His disciples as they returned from town and saw Him conversing with the Samaritan woman, at the well. When asked if He needed nourishment for His body, His response was that His meat was to do the will of the One who sent Him, and finish His (Jehovah's) work. In other words, the thing that sustained Him, energized Him, provided Him with everything He needed to carry out the tasks assigned to Him, was doing the will of the Father.

Jesus was not dependent on natural sources to provide Him with what He needed to accomplish His assignment. He was dependent on His faith. According to the definition of faith provided by the TRM/ROMI School of Ministry, "faith is unquestioning confidence and trust in the Word we had heard from God." It was His faith and obedience to fulfill His purpose, which were the nutrients that energized Him and made it possible for Him to walk in His destiny. He knew that in order to set a good example and pattern, for us, of how to be totally dependent on God, He would have to place doing the will of God as the priority in His life. Regardless of what others perceived as a deficit, He was able to maintain forward movement because His motivation was to please the Father, to accomplish and fulfill the purpose for which He had been established in the earth. Despite what appeared to be an apparent lack of adequate supply and energy, He was able to minister because His obedience proved to be a source of sustenance. When the natural nutrients and resources were not in place to carry Him on, it had to be doing the will of the Father that continued to drive Him forward, and subsequently energize Him to complete His assigned task.

It is and shall be with the remnant. Although the natural eye will consider her inadequate, understaffed, under-financed, ill-equipped according to this world's standards, she will prevail. Despite her numerical deficiencies, her faith and commitment to obediently fulfill the Father's prophetic agenda will be all she needs to walk in her destiny. These attributes of faithful obedience will not only sustain her, but they will propel her in the proper direction, at the proper time, and with the proper persons to accomplish every aspect of the will of God. He needs the remnant to succeed.

In order to help bring about the close of the age, the remnant must be single focused in trusting that God has deposited in them everything they need to succeed. Their size and physical resources, or lack thereof, are not enough to hinder them from being the vehicle God uses to complete what the conformist-Church failed to fulfill. In fact, it is exactly their lack of what the natural man considers to be necessary to achieve this monumental task, which actually positions them to be just the vessel God needs to do this. It is their apparent lack that will contribute to the onlookers recognizing that it is only by the empowerment of God

Himself that they are able to do what they do. Their lack will force people to glorify God for what they are able to do, realizing that it is He who is the force by which everything is accomplished. The faith and knowledge that the Ancient of Days is poised to provide them with every type of resource they need is the very thing that sustains the Remnant Church, and empowers her. When we speak of the remnant, we address the concept of a residue or something that remains after a larger part is taken away or separated. The remnant is the part that is designated to remain after the majority portion has been removed.

> "It is imperative that we understand that the existence of the Remnant Church is a deliberate and purposeful act of God."

The Remnant Church is not a coincidental byproduct of the conformist-Church's failure to perform. She is not a happenstance or after thought of God, as He pondered how to deal with the compromise that has been able to creep into the contemporary Church. The remnant does not exist merely because God didn't know what to do about the enemy's ability to de-claw the Church and render her powerless because of her authority being undermined by conforming to this world's standards. The remnant is not an unintentional, accidental mishap that just happens to come into existence just in the nick of time, to save God from the embarrassment of a failed strategy. It is really the polar opposite of those suppositions.

The Remnant Church is the organism that has been elected, chosen, and selected to stay behind, stay put, and continue in operation long after the conformist, deceived, compromised

Church has outlived her usefulness. She is the vehicle that the Ancient of Days has nominated to linger in the earth until the fulfillment of all things. It is imperative that we understand that the existence of the Remnant Church is a deliberate and purposeful act of God. It reflects a decision that was made in the annals of eternity. She is a group of saints that have been elected by Jehovah to continue in the apostle's doctrine long after the conformist-Church has abdicated her position of power and authority. She has been chosen to help fulfill the plan of the Father to reconcile the world to Himself, and bring the institution known as "time" to an end. Time also exists to give mankind an opportunity to escape the final judgment against evil, which will take place as God blends time into eternity. Time is a period that has been set aside for something to begin, happen, and end. It currently represents the period that God has allowed for man to once again have access to eternal life, the same eternal life he had in the Garden of Eden.

In this period allotted for the reconciliation of mankind, God has selected the Remnant Church to insure that His original purpose in establishing the Church in the earth is fulfilled. Even though the original vehicle will not bring mankind to its expected end, the conformist-Church will catapult a designated group of believers to a precipice of decision. Knowing the end from the beginning, God has decreed that a segment of the conformist-Church will remain faithful to the doctrine and purpose of the 1st century Church; it is God's ram in the bush; it's called the Remnant Church. The remnant is the part that is still in place after the completion of a process. It is the part that is still intact after all of the changes and transitions have taken place in the original structure. It is still planted and anchored in its original position, with all of its original power and virtues in place.

After God has allowed the conformist-Church to decline and settle into just a shadow of its original greatness, the Remnant Church emerges to carry out the dictates of Jehovah, and accomplish His initial purpose for the ecclesia. She rises as His representation in the midst of an evil and chaotic time. She manifests stability and power in an environment where the inhabitants of the earth are searching for a physical manifestation of the one true invisible God.

After God allows the completion of the process, which depletes the conformist-Church of all of her usefulness, the Remnant Church surges forth in the power and authority of the Apostolic Church that was birthed on the Day of Pentecost. She begins to boldly operate in the power of The Holy Spirit, as the magnet that will draw mankind to repentance before that great and terrible Day of the Lord. She remains as a designated authority of the Lord, a strong tower into which those seeking salvation can run and find refuge. The Remnant Church has not been moved off her mark; she has maintained her position and is operating exactly in the place where she has been commanded to have dominion. She has not been swayed by the winds of change or the doctrines of men; she has remained faithful to the Great Commission.

The remnant can also be said to be "the rest of;" it is the something that remains over, after the other part has been extracted. When the conformist-Church has been moved out and taken out of the way; the Remnant Church stands as that which was chosen to be separated from the conformist-Church, and designated as adequate enough to remain in content and substance as the fullness of what the original was. She has been delegated to successfully operate in the void of power and purpose which resulted from the conformist-Church's failure to fulfill her original purpose. She represents the balance, or the stability, of the essence of the Church. She functions in the fundamental nature and core values of the organism that Christ left in the earth to finish His work of reconciliation. The Remnant Church is the personification of God and operates in His Spirit to fulfill the real meaning of the word Christian. She is the physical embodiment of His character, the epitome of His love for the creation, and the exemplification of His concern for mankind, and His ultimate desire for mankind to have eternal life.

After the procedure or course of action takes place that separates the pretenders from the real, the false from the true, the weak from the strong, what is left in place, is actually of a higher quality then that from which it was taken. The Remnant Church emerges as a body which has a greater propensity to use the anointing of God, simply because it is what is left in place when the impurities of the conformist-Church are removed from the Body of Christ. She stands as a purged and pruned organism, free of defect, free of obstacles that could block the flow of the anointing, but most of all, dedicated to fully accomplish the purpose of God. She is of a higher quality because she has truly crucified her agenda. The remnant has put their agenda to death. They have not covered it, they have not masked it, they have not hidden it; they have killed it. They have completely destroyed it, lest in a situation when their flesh wants to be in control, their agenda should try to rise in opposition to God's agenda. Therefore when the imps of hades come to perpetuate compromise against God's agenda, there is nothing for them to anchor onto because every vestige of the remnant is in subjection to God's agenda. There is no wiggle room. There is no room for leaven.

So, the quality of the remnant is greater because she has a genuine predisposition to carry out God's commands. She has a greater inclination to be in total alignment with the vision of God, and will not deviate from the plan which He has instructed her to follow. While the conformist-Church has a penchant or weakness to give in to the things that will bring her acclaim, the remnant has a predilection or preference to avoid those things, and she has a tendency to only do the things that will bring glory to God. As the fire separates the dross from the gold, so the Lord's pruning process for establishing the remnant will serve as a refining and perfecting of those chosen to be the harbingers of God's peace and wrath at the end of the age. As the Father allows the winds of secular change to blow on the conformist-Church, the internal struggle she experiences will prove to be the thing that causes the remnant to be weighted down with the mantle of holiness.

As the spiritual foundation of the contemporary conformist-Church begins to crack and crumble, as the effect of compromise begins to take its toll on her, the members who accept that conforming compromise will become more visible. They will become as noticeable as the dross that floats on the molten precious ore during the refining process. They will not be as substantial as the valued gold which is hidden because of the content of its substance. The refining process will render them good for nothing, but to be separated from the valuable, prized adherents to the apostolic tenets of faith.

It is the compromised Church's struggle to accept the ways of the world or maintain the apostle's doctrine that will precipitate the separation of the remnant from the conformist. It is the battle to hold the plumb line of holiness as a standard operating procedure that will cause the rift, much like the separation that happened with serpents in the wilderness camp of Israel.

"And the people spake against God, and against Wherefore have ye brought us up out of Egypt to die in the wilderness? for there is no bread, neither is there any water; and our soul loatheth this bread. And the Lord sent fiery serpents among the people, and they bit the people much of Israel died. Therefore the people came to Moses, and said, we have sinned against the Lord, and against thee; pray unto the Lord, that He take away the serpents from us. And Moses prayed for the people. And the Lord said to Moses, Make thee a fiery serpent and set it upon a pole: and it shall come to pass, that everyone that is bitten, when he looketh upon it, shall live. And Moses made a serpent of brass, and put it upon a pole, and it came to pass, that if a serpent had bitten a man; when he beheld the serpent of brass, he lived." Numbers 21:5-9

In order for the remnant to effectively engage in end-times ministry, she must be proven, battle-ready, pressure tested Servant Warriors of Jehovah. She has to know what it means to "go through," "pray through," and "persevere." She cannot faint at the slightest test, trial, or tribulation. The remnant can ill-afford to be weak at heart. She must know how to engage in spiritual warfare, and she must have experience using her weapons, and not merely have mental knowledge of them. The Remnant Church must continually have her senses exercised to discern good and evil by reason of use, and be committed to see the war through until the end. She cannot have an "escapist mentality," but she must stand ready to see the mission through to its final conclusion. The remnant cannot be "wishy washy." They cannot be on fire and in the heat of the battle today, and tired, worn out and on the sidelines tomorrow. She must have gone through the seasoning process. The Remnant Church must be marinated in the cauldron of hardship, thereby proving and strengthening her faith. It is this "seasoning process" that establishes her as "ready" to shoulder the awesome responsibility of being an active participant in end-times ministry. This process is necessary in order for the remnant to be equipped, prepared, and organized to be geared up for the battle that is in front of her. She must have practiced using all of the weaponry at her disposal in order to be adequately prepared to vanquish her formidable foe.

Her foe is not just a run of the mill anti-God entity. He was the most powerful angel in heaven; he guarded the throne of God, and he led the angelic host in praise. He was deceitful enough to influence one-third of the angels, who only knew holiness and perfection, to follow him in an active rebellion against the Lord God Jehovah. He had the ability to persuade supernatural beings, who had no knowledge of evil, to transgress the hierarchy of heaven, and compromise their loyalty to the one true living God. Lucifer's success in getting those angels to compromise should serve as an example of just how little of a match mankind is for him, apart from the power of the Holy Ghost. This should also allow the remnant to recognize how easy it was for him to introduce compromise into the midst of the conformist-Church. These are beings who themselves are not supernatural in origin, but only have access to natural power. There is only one way mortal beings, which have been infused with the power of God, can combat and defeat this ancient foe. This foe has been waging war against the Kingdom of God from before the foundation of the earth. The remnant has to be well versed in the spiritual weapons and armament that is available to them. They must also be extremely adept at effectively using the weapons of their warfare. They must be able to receive and follow orders and instructions. They must be mature enough to trust their leadership and move synergistically as one, armed force moving in one direction, and moving with one purpose. This state of being does not happen by osmosis. It is not a condition that one accidentally stumbles into. It happens by design, and is achieved intentionally by going through the process intended to purposefully bring about this stature in the organism.

    We can also visualize the remnant to be the part of a testator's estate remaining after the satisfaction of all debts, charges, allowances, and previous devises or bequests. After every financial settlement of an estate's outstanding condition has been taken care of, there is a balance that is unused and is yet available to be used for any additional situations that have to be dealt with. This is the purpose the remnant serves: the unused portion that still has functionality. They are the unused portion that yet has value. Jesus is the testator and the Church being the estate, the picture should be clear. There is a larger portion of the Church which has been exhausted; it has been used to cope with what the Church has had to struggle against up to this point. The Remnant Church has to be careful not to stand in condemnation of tradition and denominationalism; she must guard against pride and false humility. The Remnant Church is the outgrowth of these two establishments. These portions of the testator's estate were absolutely necessary to provide the springboard from which the remnant could be launched. The fact of the matter is that had there not been any denominations or tradition, there would be no remnant. The fact that there is a remnant is a direct result of the fact that these two institutions of denomination and tradition existed and continue to exist. Since the remnant is a by-product of these things, they can ill-afford to decry them. These institutions were necessary as a foundation from which the remnant could emerge. They are the place that the remnant transitions from. If they do not exist, then the remnant has no place from which to claim its origin. Therefore, we must value the institutions of tradition and denominationalism. Although they might not be the things we need to empower us in end-times ministry, they were definitely needed as the things to launch us into end-times ministry.

> *"The Remnant Church has to be careful not to stand in condemnation of tradition and denominationalism; she must guard against pride and false humility. The Remnant Church is the outgrowth of these two establishments."*

This is the reason that we should not refer to ourselves as non-denominational; we should correctly label ourselves interdenominational. If the truth is to be told, we are truly comprised of a little bit of all of them. They have all played a part in the development of Christianity, and the growth of the Universal Church. The conformist-Church was not always conformist, she morphed into that state. The fact of the matter is that she was a powerhouse at her inception. She was walking in the power and authority of her role model, Jesus the Christ. Even in her infancy, she was a power to be reckoned with. She was actively duplicating the works she had witnessed Messiah Jesus perform. She was bold, confident, confrontational, compassionate, and committed. As she ascends and recovers from her plunge into the dark ages, she is continually being built line upon line, precept upon precept. This descent of the conformist-Church was due to her apostolic leadership being stolen by Rome as Constantine declared Christianity the official religion of the Roman Empire.

  Dr. Bill Hamon, in his magnanimous work, "The Eternal Church," succinctly describes the attention to detail the Father used, as He restored moves of His Spirit into the Church. Dr. Hamon gives us an account of how the various "movements" the Church experienced as a result of the Protestant Reformation were indicative of God bringing her back to vitality, operational functionality, and power. As God began to send wave after wave of His anointing into the Church, she began to return back to her place of origin. She began to look more and more like the 1st century apostolic body of believers who personified the image and character of Yeshua. As she climbed out of the hall of Roman Catholicism, the enemy increased his campaign to invalidate her claim to holiness and taint her testimony by constantly enticing her with the principle of compromise.

Satan interjected compromise into every facet of Christian living. From immorality to greed, from in-fighting to apathy, the enemy has attempted to thwart the growth of the Universal Church by lulling her to sleep by way of compromise. He has attempted to steal the vigor and zeal of the redeemed, by enticing them with compromise and then condemning them for giving into it. Though his efforts have been somewhat successful, the outcome was not a surprise to God.

Though the Church may have been momentarily incapacitated, she was not totally debilitated. Our God does know the end from the beginning; He is ever mindful of what we need before we need it. That's why it is called provision. It is the resource provided and put in place before the need arises for its usage. It is a product of God's anticipation of what is required to fulfill the mission, based on His omniscience, and His commitment to not allow His Word to return to Him void. This causes Him to have everything the Remnant Church needs for her success in place, exactly when she needs it. In order for the remnant to fulfill her purpose, there are "operations of the Spirit" that must be in place and available to do battle against the forces of hell. There are supernatural powers, which only God can provide, that must be utilized in this end-time battle against evil, and the evil one. There are armaments, the remnant must possess, that are specifically designed and intended to defeat the ramped-up offense of satan at the end of the age. Again, because He knows the end from the beginning, Jehovah strategically provides everything the Remnant Church needs to win the war, and places them at her disposal exactly when they need to be in place for her to bring into usage.

The righteous people of God, those in right relationship with Him, comprise the Remnant Church. In a time when there has been a major infiltration of the Church, by the devices of Lucifer, there must remain a people who are upright, honorable, virtuous, and blameless. A people that have the moral fiber to decry the "popular forms of worship" that send mixed messages to the unbelievers, and confuse them as to whether they are in church, or at the club. There must be a remnant who is dedicated to the original mission of the Church—*salvation from the penalty of sin, and deliverance from the practice of sin*. This must be the catalyst for all she does in ministry, at the end of the age. She must be focused on spiritually educating her members, and strengthening them so that they are strong enough to spiritually reproduce themselves. A people that are committed to fasting, prayer, holiness, and deliverance are a formidable foe against the kingdom of darkness. Those who have not compromised, have not conformed to the deception injected into the Church by the "prince of the power of the air," are the righteous remnant. They are those that are left over after His divine judgment. They are the ones who escape, survivors, and those who have been loosed from their bonds.

All of these aforementioned phrases are concepts expressed by Hebrew words in the Old Testament, to convey the idea of the remnant. Objects or people may be separated from a larger group by selection, assignment, or destruction. The Ancient of Days views the components of the conformist-Church and makes a collective choice of people to comprise the remnant. He makes an allocation of the resources in the conformist-Church to those people who have decided not to deviate from the original purpose for which the Church was left in the earth. Jehovah delegates His righteous people to carry on the ministry and work of His Son. He deputizes them [in a manner of speaking] to execute His judgments in the earth. He appoints the remnant; He entrusts and authorizes them to serve as His ambassador, or envoy. They become His agent, and a duly authorized emissary with the ability to speak on His behalf, and decree His rulings and decisions.

    The Remnant Church exists because Elohim has designated her to exist. The only wise God has chosen her, selected her, and elected her to operate as the portion of the body of believers that helps restore the Church back to her original place of prominence. He does this by obliterating the conformist-Church; He eliminates her influence. He shifts the world's focus from her by reducing her importance to nothing. He wipes out her ability to speak on His behalf, and bequeaths that to the remnant. When we speak of the Father's annihilation of the conformist-Church, we are merely talking about His intent to extinguish, smother, snuff out and turn off her ability to distract unbelievers, and believers alike. We are referring to His strategy to prohibit the conformist-Church from presenting a false image of Christianity. We are alluding to His plan to allow the true image of His Church to shine forth by removing the conformist-Church from the spotlight, and placing His chosen vessel that accurately reflects who He is at center-stage. God is able to do this by devastation of the character of the conformist-Church; He exposes her for who she is. He ruins her reputation and wrecks her influence by shifting the world's attention to focus on the group that correctly represents Him: The Remnant Church.

The God of Abraham, Isaac, and Jacob must orchestrate demolition of the conformist-Church. He must knock down and pull down the foundations and traditions which are the result of the Roman government's successful overthrow, if you will; of the apostolic leadership Jehovah, through Jesus Christ, set in place to govern the Church. As previously stated, when Rome embraced Christianity as the state-religion, she was able to wrestle the governance of the Church from the hands of the apostles.[1] She replaced apostolic leadership with secular leadership, and thus set in motion the events that began to thrust the 1st century Church into her decline. God must undo this. He must demolish the effect of the conformist-Church; He must destroy her influence. What is left over when He does this is the residue or remnant, the Remnant Church.

The remnant can also be described as those who remain after an epidemic, war, or some other type of cataclysmic event. What happened when Rome incorporated Jewish Christianity into Roman government can be seen as an epidemic. An epidemic is a plague.

- ◊ It is a disease that is accompanied by infection.
- ◊ It is a curse, an outbreak, with the subsequent eruption of a rash which is contagious.
- ◊ It is communicable, transmittable and has the ability to contaminate and pollute.
- ◊ It is also associated with the corruption of that which is whole

and healthy.
◊ It is often seen as a scourge: a blight or bane that is endemic in nature, and viewed as something that is a common, widespread and extensively deadly disease.

This sums up what happened when the apostles, who were left in charge to administer the Church, were replaced by a government that removed the concept of conversion as a result of repentance. Rome replaced the foundation of repentance and baptism by immersion with the notion that one could become a Christian simply by being sprinkled with water, or being born into a family that was already a part of the Church. This practice lives up to all the references we made to the epidemic which ensued, or developed, when Rome took over the governance of the 1st century Church. The Great I Am must totally decimate the negative impact that the loss of apostolic leadership had on the Church. The way He will do this is to take the conformist-Church off of center-stage and replace her with His delegated authority and designated representative...the Remnant Church.

The contemporary conformist-Church is on an inescapable road to an internal conflict. It is headed into an inevitable war within itself that will serve as a line of demarcation between those who desire to maintain the tenets upon which the Church was birthed, and those who are open to accept the spiritually compromising ways of the world. The ways of the world are those which are designed to make the Church appealing to people who want to be self-indulgent, yet claim to be submitted to God.

CHAPTER ONE: THE REMNANT

One of the main pillars of Christianity rests upon our conscious decision to abdicate the "throne of our life," and instead, allow God to sit in that place of authority. This war focuses on our willingness to do the things that are pleasing to Him, in deference to doing the things that give us pleasure, and making pleasing Him our number one priority.

1. It will be a universal general war.
2. It will not be isolated to a particular country or culture.
3. It will not be relegated to a certain economic or social class.
4. It will affect the entire Body of Christ.
5. It will serve as a sword to divide the holy from the carnal; the surrendered from the self-serving, and those committed to the "old" ways from those intent on replacing those old holy values with "new" ones; that are more current and socially acceptable.

One might even call those new ways "politically correct." In order for God's Word to be fulfilled and His agenda to be accomplished, there must be a "great falling away" from the principles of faith upon which the Church was established. In order for prophecy to be fulfilled there must be an abandonment of the apostolic principles that founded the Church. We must remember that the apostle's doctrine, which served as the basis for these principles, was merely a duplication of the instruction they had received from Christ. Those principles sustained the Church through the persecution of the Roman government. Those are the same principles that helped her through the Protestant Reformation. Through the subsequent ages, as God began to restore her back to her original state, it has been these same principles that built her, and are now the target of the contemporary conformist-Church. These principles are in the cross-hairs of conformity, because they stand as a promoter of holiness, instead of an advocate for the endorsement of moderation. This upcoming civil war will be known as The Great Apostasy.

The Remnant Church represents the fully restored Church. In order for the Church to be translated, she must first be restored to her original place of ultimate dominance. In order for Jesus to receive her and offer her up to the Father, she must first be in the position where she is unified. She must be a measure of the stature of the fullness of Christ. The remnant represents the culmination of the restoration of all of the doctrines, truths and spiritual experiences with which God will bless the Church. He has been constantly restoring her through all the different "movements," which have helped to move the Church out of her decline. The Protestant Reformation Movement, the Holiness Movement, the Pentecostal Movement, the Charismatic Movement, and the Prophetic-Apostolic Movement comprise these moves of God.

> "Just as Israel experienced a judgment for their apostasy, so the conforming Church will be evicted and thrown out of her place of world influence."

The great apostasy is a great rebellion against God Himself. It is an aggressive climatic revolt against God that will prepare the way for the appearance of the man of sin.

CHAPTER ONE: THE REMNANT

"Let no man deceive you by any means: for that day shall not come, except there come a falling away first, and that man of sin be revealed, the son of perdition. Who opposseth and exalteth himself above all that is called God, or that is worshipped, so that he as God sitteth in the Temple of God, showing himself that he is God." II Thesselonians 2:3-4

The great apostasy represents a specific act of rebellion that embodies the supreme opposition by the forces of evil to the things of God. Satanic deception, which caused the fall of man, will characterize the end of the age. Satan is the one who deceives the whole world [2] and is the power behind the beast and the false prophet.[3] The time is coming when professing Christians will reject the truth to embrace the doctrines proclaimed by false teachers.[4] Let us examine this term, "apostasy." According to Webster's Dictionary, apostasy is the renunciation or abandonment of a former loyalty. It is renouncing, rejecting, repudiating, or denying something to which you previously had allegiance or faithfulness. It is an abandonment or desertion of something to which at one time you had devotion and fidelity. The result is that you end up leaving behind and neglecting an ideal to which you had previously been committed.

The Old Testament speaks of it in terms of falling away, such as deserting to a foreign king. Associated ideas include: religious unfaithfulness; rebellion; cast away; trespass, and backsliding. As we examine the Scriptures,[5] we see numerous accounts of Abraham's descendant's unfaithfulness to Jehovah. Time and time again, they cast away the worship of the Great I Am, and exchanged it for the worship of the false gods of their neighbors in surrounding lands. They constantly rebelled against His ways, trespassed His laws and statutes, and were commonly referred to as "backsliders." In a manner of speaking, they deserted their king and sovereign, and cast their lot with the great deceiver. They chose the guardian of the throne, as opposed to choosing the One who sits upon the throne. Although the word "apostasy" was not used to describe their condition, it certainly applied. The definition of apostasy accurately connotes what these Hebrews were guilty of doing. They were abandoning and leaving behind their foundation principles, for that which did not have the power to sustain them.

The prophets picture Israel's history as one filled with apostasy. They continually turned from God to "other gods." As a result of their apostasy, they experienced "exile." Until recently, 1948 to be specific, the Jewish nation was still experiencing the result of being scattered to the nations. They had been dispossessed of their land, and had no homeland to speak of. They were scattered to the wind, separated from their inheritance, the land of Canaan, and were a people without a country. As a result of their disloyalty, their sovereign had released them from their place of prominence.

The natural consequence of abandoning your king is to be banished, sent away, and separated from the benefits associated with being under his covering, or being a part of his kingdom/government. When one chooses to reject or deny the government standards to which they had a former allegiance, it should not be a surprise when they are deported, and separated from their previous position. Just as Israel experienced a judgment for their apostasy,

CHAPTER ONE: THE REMNANT

so the conforming Church will be evicted and thrown out of her place of world influence. She must be forced out and pushed out of the way to make room for the Remnant Church. The remnant must have room to fully operate in the power of the Spirit without being in competition with another group posing as the lawful representative of the Almighty. Therefore, the conforming Church must be ejected out of her place as the mouthpiece of Jehovah. The Father has to set her aside, not only because she has conformed, but also because she has failed to maintain adherence to the principles of holiness, upon which the Church was founded. Generally speaking, in the New Testament, apostasy is considered to be the act of rebelling against, forsaking, abandoning, or falling away from what one has believed. It is condemned in the Epistle of Jude.

> *"So I want to remind you, though you already know these things, that Jesus[b] first rescued the nation of Israel from Egypt, but later he destroyed those who did not remain faithful. And I remind you of the angels who did not stay within the limits of authority God gave them but left the place where they belonged. God has kept them securely chained in prisons of darkness, waiting for the great Day of Judgment. And don't forget Sodom and Gomorrah and their neighboring towns, which were filled with immorality and every kind of sexual perversion. Those cities were destroyed by fire and serve as a warning of the eternal fire of God's judgment." Jude 5-7 (NLT)*

Apostasy is derived from the Greek word apostasia. The New Testament speaks of it in terms of, "to stand away from." The Greek noun only occurs twice in the New Testament;[6] though it is not translated as "apostasy."

"But the Jewish believers here in Jerusalem have been told that you are teaching all the Jews who live among the Gentiles to turn their backs on the laws of Moses. They've heard that you teach them not to circumcise their children or follow other Jewish customs." Acts 21:21

"Let no man deceive you by any means: for that day shall not come, except there come a falling away first, and that man of sin be revealed, the son of perdition;" II Thessalonians 2:3

> *"Satan's strategy is to make the Church comfortable adopting a policy of moderation, founded in the principle of self-satisfaction."*

II Thessalonians addresses those who believed that the Day of the Lord had already come. However, Paul was clarifying that an apostasy would proceed that Day. He was letting them know that one of the telltale signs the Day of the Lord was upon them would be the apostasy and the revealing of the son of perdition. In I Timothy. 4:1, the Spirit had explicitly revealed this falling away from the faith.

"Now the Spirit speaketh expressly, that in the latter times some shall depart from the faith, giving heed to seducing spirits, and doctrines of devils;" I Timothy 4:1

In latter times, such apostasy will involve doctrinal deception, moral insensitivity, and ethical departures from

God's truth.[7] God is acutely aware of the fact that the enemy is intent upon deceiving the Church. Our foe is deliberately introducing seductive doctrines designed to sway the Church from the principles of holiness. Satan's strategy is to make the Church comfortable adopting a policy of moderation, founded in the principle of self-satisfaction. His desire is to manipulate the Church into a state where pleasing God is equated with pleasing ourselves. He wants to convince the Church that it is justifiable behavior to not be so rigid and adherent to the call to holiness, that it doesn't take "all that." It is the conforming Church's acceptance of these principles that is the very thing that disqualifies her to be the conduit of the "power of the Spirit" necessary to accomplish the end-time mandate for the Church. It is exactly why the conforming Church must be moved aside to make room for the Remnant Church; she must be exiled in order for the remnant to emerge.

Apostasy is a Biblical concept that has fueled a lot of debate. The biblical warnings against it should cause us to recognize that while God does have the ability to keep us, man still has a "free will." That free will positions man to have the ability to ignore God's commands, and potentially reject His salvation and dictates. There must be a realization that apostasy, by nature, is subject to a cause and effect relationship. The actions one takes, or doesn't take, produces a direct effect on the status of the relationship. When one freely chooses to disregard the standards by which their organism was birthed and by which it grew, there are consequences.

When one chooses to compromise the morals and ethics by which the Church has maintained her reputation and integrity, as the delegated authority and designated representative of God, one leaves themselves vulnerable and exposed. In reality, one has positioned themselves to experience the judgment of God. This judgment might conceivably look like being moved aside, so that a more qualified representative can occupy that position of honor.

There is an inherent danger in religious unfaithfulness that necessitates exile. When one does not correctly reflect the values of their sovereign, one for whom you are supposed to be an ambassador, there is no justification for allowing that entity to continue being seen as a legal representative of said sovereign. While the contemporary conforming Church was duly charged and elected to be Jehovah's envoy, by exercising her "free will" to accept the devil's compromise, she voluntarily made herself a candidate for exile, and ultimately replacement. While "free will" is a wonderful gift given to us by the Father, it also poses a threat to those who misuse it, or use it without the proper filter. Since man is not an android or robot, there has to be a conscious exercise of free will to maintain adherence to the faith that was passed on to us by the founding apostolic fathers.

The conforming Church has to either decide to repent and return to her apostolic origins, or face the penalty of apostasy. Apostasy ends up with her being placed aside and no longer being used as the harbinger of the Gospel message. If the conforming Church does not exercise her free will to return to the position occupied by the 1st century Church, she leaves God no alternative but to replace her with a Church that will maintain His standards. She forces the Father to cause a division to take place within her ranks or an extraction so to speak. What remains is a Church that refuses to be seduced into compromising the old landmarks that have come to frame the integrity of the Body of Christ.

This extraction is known as the Remnant Church. There has always been a remnant. All throughout the Holy Scriptures one has always been able to find the concept and example of the remnant. Both of the divided kingdoms of Judah and Israel can be said to have experienced circumstances which qualified them to be classified as having a remnant.[8] While this thought is typically associated with the nation of Israel, there are specific examples of individuals that can also be pointed to as fitting the classification as a remnant. Noah and his family can be said to have been survivors, remnants, of the divine judgment God executed against the whole of humanity when He smote the earth with the Great Flood.[9] The exact same thing can be said of Lot, as he escaped the destruction of Sodom and Gomorrah.[10]

We dare not forget Jacob's family as they fled to Egypt to find refuge from the famine and drought that had plagued humanity.[11] This small surviving group became the nucleus of Hebrews that God used to fulfill His prophetic promise to Abram. He assured faithful Abram that the sign, that Jehovah had cut a covenant with him, would be the enslavement of Abram's descendants in a foreign land for over 400 years.[12] While Joseph's brothers didn't have to sell him into slavery in order for God to position him as the second most powerful man in the then known world, it was God ordained for them to do so. They unwittingly helped God's covenant promise to Abram to come into fruition. Elijah and the 7000 faithful followers of Yahweh represent yet another example of the remnant, as they would not bow their knees to Baal and the wicked King Ahab and Queen Jezebel.[13] The whole nation was steeped in Baal worship, yet there was a faithful remnant to the God of Abraham, Isaac, and Jacob. Can we fail to mention Daniel,[14] Shadrach, Meshach, and Abednego; I think not.[15]

There are countless other heroes of the faith, who stand as an example of those who were left over, escaped, survived or were loosed from their bonds either by selection, assignment or destruction of the larger group. They stand as monumental pillars of faith and testimonies to the concept of the remnant.

> *"God is merely looking for a Church that will stay faithful to the assignment for which she was chosen."*

Whether they were selected or assigned, they serve to demonstrate to us that God doesn't need a great crowd. Rather, a faithful few, such as Gideon's three hundred.[16] The prophet Isaiah is one of the strongest vocal proponents of "the remnant." He was so committed to the idea that he named one of his sons Shear-Jashub, meaning "a remnant shall return."[17]

Isaiah understood that while exile, as a consequence of disobedience, was inescapable, God always allows the opportunity for repentance and redemption. Let me be absolutely clear of this one thing, when God exiles the conforming Church, it is not to destruction with no hope of redemption. It is merely a process where He shifts the emphasis, and world attention, from the Church that has been seduced into compromise. His desire is to make the non-conformist-Church, which has chosen to remain true to the tenets of the 1st century Church, the primary focus of this world. If the conforming Church sees the error of her ways, and repents, she can be grafted into the remnant.

God is merely looking for a Church that will stay faithful to the assignment for which she was chosen. God is willing to allow the truly repentant to be restored back to usefulness. While there will be some in the conforming Church that will never repent, there will be those who yield to the conviction of The Holy Spirit and return to their first love. God's intention has always been to have "a people" that would voluntarily serve and love Him. Many of Isaiah's remnant passages are closely tied to the future king who would be the majestic ruler of those who would seek His mercies, the Messiah. These passages have a strong eschatological thrust, expecting future generations to be the remnant. Other passages looked to the remnant to be in Isaiah's day. However, the passages in the latter part of the book have a very evident future orientation. They intimate that there would be a new people, a new community, a new nation, and an extremely strong faith in one God.

The Messianic Jews and the 1st century New Testament Church are an example of the concept of the remnant. As Israel moved from the dispensation of Law through the dispensations of Grace and Kingdom, there had to be a new group that would emerge from the old. There had to be something that was taken out of the old group as a remainder or left over. Though Israel had progressed from the Dispensation of Promise through the Dispensation of The Law, she still had not reached her final destination. She still had not evolved into the form necessary to catapult God's body of believers to the end of the age. One has to recognize that in order for a remnant to emerge, there must be an erosion of sorts in the original body.

The changes that happened in Judaism and the Jews' strict adherence to the Law were necessary for God's plan to be fulfilled. Her legalism and legalistic religious practices were necessary in order for the Messianic Church to be birthed. Those practices were the reason that certain Jews were willing to receive John's baptism of repentance, and subsequently sever their relationship with the temple and the nation of Israel. Those Jews that stepped into the Jordan to be baptized of John knew that they were voluntarily separating themselves from the main body of the Jewish community, and that they would be ostracized because of their decision. They didn't cower in fear, as they readily made themselves the remnant. They were those who were separated from the larger body, yet had a more powerful relationship with their God, Jehovah.

While the Jews, that group who had exclusivity when it came to relationship with Jehovah, were moved aside in order for the focus to shift onto the 1st century Church; they were not completely thrown away. The Jews continue to be God's chosen people, even today. The time clock for our world centers upon them. Apocalyptic prophecy revolves around that small Middle Eastern nation. In addition to all of that, they still have the ability to be saved. God has not forgotten them, and has made provision for them to repent and be grafted into the Remnant Church.

The Gentile Church is supposed to provoke the Jews to jealousy, and make them want to enter into the same covenant relationship with Jehovah, which the Gentile Church has. The Ancient of Days, the God of the Hebrews, is simply amazing, and

His love for His creation is unsurpassed.

The greater number of the other prophets may not have been as explicit as Isaiah was in their usage of the term "remnant." Nevertheless, their works are replete with the idea that only a few of the Jews would survive judgment, as a result of their repentance, and God would use them to raise up a new community or nation. Amos, Micah, Ezekiel, Jeremiah, and Zechariah[18] all prophetically alluded to the notion that there would be a small group of leftovers that would survive the exile, return to the Promised Land, resettle Jerusalem, rebuild the Temple, and establish God's new community of covenant believers. Jehovah always had and will always have a "remnant."

"To every thing there is a season, and a time to every purpose under the heaven:"

Ecclesiastes 3:1

Chapter Two

Why a Remnant Church?

According to Dr. Bill Hamon, author of "The Eternal Church," there is a process that the Church has gone through since her inception. It is a process marked by an inception full of power and authority. Through a series of events, she declined in both areas, and began to see a restoration to her initial state as she experienced the Protestant Reformation.

Dr. Hamon's work leads one to believe that the Church

must be fully restored before Jesus comes back to offer her up to the Father. There were some foundational spiritual truths and experiences that were lost as the Church slipped into her "dark ages." Without going into the causes of those losses here, we will say that they were an integral component of the fiber and fabric that vested the Church in her power. These doctrines, truths, and spiritual experiences were active ingredients in the recipe that yielded the signs and wonders that gave the Church credence. They are the very things that God wants to bring to the forefront in the Remnant Church, as a means of validating her, and substantiating her right to operate in the earth as His delegated authority and designated representative. They are components that are currently missing in the conforming, deceived, compromised Church, and must be operational and visible in the Remnant Church.

If the remnant is going to garner the attention it needs to serve as a magnet for the "final harvest," these 1st century apostolic signs and wonders must be fully operational and noticeably visible. There is a restoration of lost doctrines, truths, and spiritual experiences that must take place for the Remnant Church to justify her existence as the legal replacement of the conforming Church. The remnant cannot simply decry the conforming Church's seduction and claim to be her replacement without a demonstration of signs, wonders, power, and authority. Otherwise, why would there be a need for a remnant? Why would we attempt to replace that which already has longevity, without being able to justify the replacement based on operational functionality? In order for the Father to substantiate the need to move the conforming Church out of the limelight and shift the focus onto a more qualified spokesperson, He must endow that replacement with the virtue that will cause it to be a true reflection of His character and His power. There is only one reason for there to be a Remnant Church, and that is to fulfill purpose and accomplish what the conforming Church could not fulfill, and failed to accomplish. Thus, the Remnant Church must exist as a fully functional and operational organism; reflecting the character of God and the 1st century Apostolic Church. If the remnant fails to do this, she is guilty of fraud, character assassination, and spiritual homicide. Hence, the Remnant Church cannot afford to be a replica of the conforming, compromised Church it is intended to replace.

As we examine the notion of a Remnant Church, we must first understand the how, the why, the origin, and birth of the 1st century New Testament Church. Many will tell us that the Church was birthed on the Day of Pentecost, when the Father made The Holy Spirit available to dwell within the creation. No longer would the Spirit of God be dispatched from heaven to rest upon an individual person to perform a specific task, but now God's Spirit would be available to all of creation on an on-going basis. What about Jesus breathing The Holy Spirit into His disciples on Resurrection Day? We will address this fact a little later on. However, we must consider that fact. While the actual birth of the Church may be a topic for conversation, we can be assured of this one thing, the Day of Pentecost certainly represents the day that the Church became a noticeable physical reality. We can definitely mark this as the day that the Holy Spirit of God became available to ethnic Jew and non-ethnic Jew alike. As we consider the Church's birth through the eyes of the Spirit, we will have to concede that she was birthed in the eons of eternity; long before the foundation of the world.

"Blessed be the God and Father of our Lord Jesus Christ, who hath blessed us with all spiritual blessings in heavenly places in Christ: According as He has chosen us in Him before the foundation of the world, that we should be holy and without blame before Him in love." Ephesians 1:3-4

After the fall, the Messianic race (descendants of Abraham, the Jews) was born and continued in existence; in order to bring forth the Messiah. God's chosen people, the Hebrews, were selected to be the seed through which the Father would redeem creation. God's plan to reconnect the creation to Himself centered on creating a group into which He could deposit the inhabitants who freely exercised their will to worship Him, and receive His free gift of salvation. That group, or body, is known as the universal Church, the ecclesia, the called-out ones. The vessel in which these inhabitants were initially housed, known as "the Church," was first made available to and comprised of His chosen people; the Jews. Long before the fall; long before the Tower of Babel; long before the separation of the races, based on similarity of speech; Jesus was predestined to be a Jew. The original recipients of God's extension of grace to mankind, based on mankind's need for redemption, were always going to be the descendants of Noah's son Shem. The choice of the Hebrew nation to be the progenitors of the patriarchs and the Messiah was not an after-thought of God; as He decided how to deal with what happened in the Garden of Eden. Messiah

Jesus was always predestined to be of Jewish descent; a practicing Jew.

    The 1st century New Testament Church was always predestined to be an outgrowth of Judaism. Since our God knows the end from the beginning; none of what happens in the affairs of men is a surprise to Him. We must understand that the spiritual container which God had designed to hold those who responded to His call for repentance and conversion is the place that He commissioned the Messiah to create; it is known as the Church. This spiritual container was first made available to the descendants of Abraham, Isaac, and Jacob.[19] It is the receptacle for those whom God has mercifully spared from the eternal wrath which is to come upon the inhabitants of the world; who refuse to receive God's free gift of salvation. That receptacle originated out of the Jewish people, was shared with the Gentile world, and will ultimately stand as the vessel that once again houses God's chosen people; when all of Israel shall be saved.

"And so all Israel shall be saved: as it is written: There shall come out of Sion the Deliverer, and shall turn away ungodliness from Jacob." Romans 11: 26

    The Church is built upon the foundation of the apostles and prophets; Jesus Christ Himself being the Chief Cornerstone.[20] The government of the body of believers who worship Jehovah had moved from Mt. Sinai to Mt. Zion. There had been a transition from the Old Covenant to the New Covenant. God had moved His dwelling place from the Temple in Jerusalem to bodies of men and women; their bodies had become the temple of The

Holy Spirit. Even though the New Covenant supersedes the Old Covenant, it exists just as Jesus did. Messiah stated that He didn't come to do away with the Law; He came to fulfill the Law. While the New Covenant brings fullness to the Old Covenant, it does not invalidate nor disinherit the recipients of the Old Covenant. The New Covenant offers entrance to the participants of the Old Covenant, while simultaneously offering admittance to those who previously had no access to the provisions of the Old Covenant. Again, we worship the God of the Hebrews, the God of the Jews. We have accepted a Jewish Messiah, and we belong to the Messianic Jewish body of believers; known as the Church. We have been grafted into her!

What about the early Church? Let's talk about her for a moment. During her first three hundred years, she was governed by Jewish apostles. She was the object of massive persecution, and the slaughter of thousands of Christians. Perhaps even hundreds of thousands of Christians were slaughtered. The fact is that the Roman Empire, under which the Church was birthed, outlawed Christianity from 100 A.D. until 313 A.D. We don't really know what happened between 68 A.D. and 100 A.D. because there was no written Church history during that time period. In fact, there was no written record of the Church for the fifty years that followed Paul's death. Judaism, the Jewish faith from which the Church was born, also even participated in her early persecution. According

> *"While the New Covenant brings fullness to the Old Covenant, it does not invalidate nor disinherit the recipients of the Old Covenant."*

to the Book of Acts, we do know that after Pentecost, there was major persecution of the Church by the Jews; which is evidenced by the young zealous Pharisee named Saul. We also find the first recorded martyr of the New Testament Church, Steven, coming by the hands of the original body of people, the Jews, which had produced the remnant Church of the 1st century. We find the earliest writing of the Church fathers around 120 A.D. So, we can see that the early Church suffered massive persecution under the Roman government, and under the religious organization known as Judaism.

The last recorded persecution of the Church by the Roman Empire happened between 303 A.D. and 310 A.D. That remnant 1st century New Testament Church that was birthed out of Judaism, under the watch of the Roman Empire, had persecution as a tool that helped her maintain the integrity of her membership. No one would claim membership to an organization that had the potential to be responsible for causing one to lose their life; unless they were serious about their commitment to Christ. Being a part of that 1st century New Testament remnant was not popular, convenient, or glamorous. It was taken very seriously, and was not considered something that was "én vogue." Membership had its privileges, but it also had its costs. The persecution that the remnant received at the hands of the religious body that birthed her, along with the onslaught from the secular government which kept her under thumb, served as a screening filter to help determine those who were serious about changing their lifestyle. However, all of that was about to change due to the Battle at the Stone Milvian Bridge, at the Tiber River. On October 27, 312 A.D., just outside of

Rome, facing his enemy Maxentius, tradition tells us that Emperor Constantine had a vision as he was about to go into battle.

As the sun was setting, he saw a vision of a cross; with the caption of, "in this sign conquer" written above it. As a result, he fought that battle under the banner of Christianity, and won. We must note however that as he recounted the vision, the description that he gave of the cross was actually that of the Egyptian occult sign known as an ankh.[21] It was this very image that he had placed on the shields of his soldiers. After his victory, Constantine declared himself a Christian and sprinkled his troops in baptism.[22] Subsequently, Constantine made Christianity the religion of his court and encouraged his subjects to embrace it as a religion. The aristocrats and wealthy persons refused to do so, and as a result, Constantine moved his capital from Rome to Byzantium and renamed it Constantinople. This became the capital of the new Christian empire. Invariably, this led to a conflict between Rome and Constantinople for the role of the leadership of Christendom. This eventually resulted in the formation of the Eastern Orthodox Church and the Western Roman Catholic Church.

In 313 A.D. Emperor Constantine passed the now famous "Edict of Toleration" and the "Edict of Milan." In these pieces of legislation, Constantine sanctioned the practice of Christianity in the Roman Empire, made Christian worship a lawful act, and ceased all persecution of Christianity by the Roman Empire. It was this very act that represented a spiritual coup, and began the process to wrestle the leadership of Christianity from the hands of the Jewish apostles; to whom the Christ had left in charge.

This was the beginning of the formalized Church of Rome. It signaled a dominance of Roman government over the affairs of the Church. This dominance lasted unopposed for twelve hundred years; until the Protestant Reformation of the 15th century. After robbing the apostolic Jewish leadership of their governance of the 1st century New Testament Remnant Church, the next fifteen centuries of Christianity were practiced under the auspices of some form of Roman Catholicism. To make matters worse for the spiritual remnant 1st century Church, some seventy years later, the Roman Emperor Theodosius mandated Christianity to be the state religion of the Roman Empire. His decree forced all Roman subjects to formally accept Christianity in order to maintain their citizenship, hold public office, and conduct business in the Roman Empire. This single act undermined the notions of voluntary repentance and conversion, conviction of sin, spiritual rebirth, and a transformed lifestyle. These things were no longer necessary to become, or live as a Christian. Theodosius also forcibly suppressed all other religions and prohibited idol worship.[23]

    The 1st century New Testament Remnant Church had become a political organization that reflected the spirit and pattern of the Imperial Roman Empire. In order to appease some pagans who had forcibly been made to accept Christianity as the "state religion", some compromises were made. Some traditional Jewish holidays were replaced with pagan holidays; while other pagan holidays were merely thrust upon the Church. One of notable mention is Christmas. The Roman sun-worshippers celebrated the birthday of the Sun-god on December 25th. To maintain this holiday for the pagan Romans, who were forced into

Christianity, the new Church headed by the Roman government substituted the celebration of Christ's birthday on this day. Another example is how Constantine officially recognized and named the weekly meeting day for the Christians "the venerable day of the sun." We now call it Sunday; this day versus the traditional days that the Jews celebrated Sabbath; being Friday evening into Saturday evening.[24]

So, what started as a pure remnant, from a tainted religion that failed to recognize her Messiah, was transformed into a deceived compromised body. There was also a major circumstance that contributed to the mutation that happened as a result of the exchange in Church leadership; from the hands of the apostles to the hands of the Roman government. You have to brace yourselves to understand the significance of what I'm about to share with you.

"In the city of Antioch, in Syria, true believers were making 'exact' copies of the original manuscripts. From Antioch the Christians sent missionaries down to Egypt to teach the people living in Alexandria; the second largest city in the world. This was located in the land of Isis (the Queen of Heaven) and Horus (the Sun god). At that time it was the seat of Baal worship. Some of the world's greatest minds were living in Alexandria. These men were proud of their great wisdom. They called themselves 'Gnostics.' [25] *These Gnostics formed a school of religion and philosophy; that became the 'Center of Christian Learning and Culture."*

However, they didn't believe in a real heaven or hell. When they got hold of the Bible manuscripts they started making changes. A great student, Origen, became head of this school.

CHAPTER TWO: WHY A REMNANT CHURCH?

He didn't believe that Jesus was God Almighty, so he and others chopped I John 5:7 out of the scriptures. He was an Arian, he believed Jesus was a lesser God. He was mightily used by satan to corrupt Bible manuscripts.[26]

Constantine, who still secretly worshipped the sun god, ordered a man named Eusebius (the Bishop of Caesarea) to make him fifty Bibles. Eusebius had a choice of using the Greek manuscripts from Alexandria or from Antioch; to make up his fifty Greek Bibles. Since Eusebius believed the same way Origen did, he did not use the manuscripts from Antioch. Rather, he used the corrupted manuscripts from Egypt to make his Bibles for the Roman Catholic Church.[27] The Latin Vulgate Bible, written by Jerome, (Bible for the Roman Catholic Church) came out of the fifty Bibles made up by Eusebius. This became the official Bible for all Roman Catholics; all others were outlawed.[28] This is a sad commentary on the history of the 1st century New Testament Remnant Church transition into Roman Catholicism.

Another great change that affected the compromised, deceived Church that came out of the apostolically governed 1st century New Testament Remnant Church is mind boggling. The pagans were allowed to bring their statues and idols of Semiramis (the Queen of Heaven) and Nimrod (Baal, the Sun god) into the Church. The names were changed to the Virgin Mary, Queen of Heaven, and little baby Jesus. Baal worship, started by Semiramis and her husband-son Nimrod had successfully moved into the Roman Catholic institution. An interesting note is that by 1950, the Roman Catholic Church had raised the Virgin Mary to a goddess with the power to be co-savior and co-redeemer with

Christ; exactly like Semiramis. The Doctrine of the Immaculate Conception says Mary was born without original sin—1854; The Dogma of the Assumption of Mary into heaven means she never died—1950.[29]

The Bible clearly forbids the worship of the Queen of Heaven in the 7th and 44th chapters of Jeremiah. Just for clarity's sake, we need to take a closer look at the origin of Baal worship. Another sad commentary is what happened to the 15th century New Testament Remnant Church, which was formed as a result of the Protestant Reformation. She also became a deceived compromised body; necessitating the emergence of an end-times Remnant Church.

We now stand at that precipice; poised and ready for the remnant to stand up and be counted. We will examine the transition of the apostolically governed 1st century New Testament Remnant Church to the Roman governed 3rd century Church. We will then follow her descent and subsequent ascent from the 15th century Church. We ultimately will look at her progression to the end-times Remnant Church. As we follow her journey, we will simultaneously examine the nation of Israel, and the impact she has had on the world. With great detail, we will examine the relationship between the Remnant Church and the nation of Israel.

Paul makes mention of the concept of the "remnant" to the New Testament Church.[30] However, we are mindful that when he did, he was speaking of covenant promises made to ethnic Jews.

"I say the truth in Christ, I lie not, my conscience also, bearing me witness in the Holy Ghost, That I have great heaviness and continual sorrow in my heart. For

CHAPTER TWO: WHY A REMNANT CHURCH?

I could wish that myself were accursed from Christ for my brethren, my kinsmen according to the flesh: Who are Israelites; to whom pertaineth the adoption, and the glory, and the covenants, and the giving of the law, and the service of God, and the promises; Whose are the fathers, and of whom as concerning the flesh Christ came, who is over all, God blessed forever. Amen."Romans 9:1-5

He quotes Isaiah as an assurance to the Christian community living in Rome.[31] He reminds them that Yahweh's covenant promise is yet extended to His chosen people, the Jews.[32] Even though the Jews had refused to accept their Messiah, Jesus of Nazareth, God still had intentions on making salvation, deliverance from the works of the devil, available to the nation of Israel.[33]

As we look all around us, we see Jews everywhere. Orthodox Jews, Hassidic Jews, Reformed Jews, Conservative Jews, Messianic Jews; there are all kinds of Jews everywhere. They yet remain God's chosen people. Contrary to that false teaching of "Replacement Theology," God did not replace His covenant choice of the Jews with the Church. While the Church may "represent spiritual Israel," God's intention yet remains to honor the covenant He made with the Jewish nation. The Church is merely a branch. She did not replace the root; she was grafted into the root. God will use the Gentile branch to make the Jewish root jealous enough to lay claim on the free gift that was originally intended for the descendants of Abraham, Isaact, and Jacob.[34] [35]

Eventually, the Jews will realize what they have forfeited and come running to the feet of the Master; begging to be embraced and received by The Beloved.[36] Paul, who had formerly been a chief

> "Contrary to that false teaching of 'Replacement Theology,' God did not replace His covenant choice of the Jews with the Church."

persecutor of the Church, was reminding the saints in Rome that even though there was concern about the fate of the Jewish nation, and their decision not to receive Jesus of Nazareth as the Messiah; there was still a reason to hope for salvation. The idea that there would be a portion of those chosen people who would still be redeemed in spite of the nation's rejection of Christ, was directly associated with the idea of there being a remnant.

In a time when the majority of the Jews had actively and consciously decided to refuse acceptance of Jehovah's answer to the problem of the "sin nature," there was still a remnant according to God's grace. This remnant represented an assurance that God will always leave Himself a "witness." He will always allow a portion to remain who will reflect His nature and purpose. God elects a group to represent Him in accordance to their possession of the holiness and integrity necessary to influence non-believers to accept the free gift of salvation; in all of its fullness and with all of its benefits. God will always have a group that will not bow to the pressure of the world to have the Church conform to "worldly mores and values." There will always be a remnant that will maintain the faith handed down to us by the saints, and not succumb to the deceptive devices of satan.

There will always be a group of "leftovers" who will not bow their knee to Baal. This just serves as another example to illustrate for us that although the Church is the recipient of some of the covenant promises God makes in His Word; she is only a recipient because of her relationship with the Jews. It is only because the Church has been made members of the commonwealth of Israel that she can boast of inclusion into these provisions of grace. Despite the winds of change that blow upon the ecclesia, there will always be a remnant that stays the course, and remains true to the model that was left in the earth by the Christ, and His chosen leadership.

Why the concept of a Remnant Church? I am painfully aware that the concept of the "remnant church" does not appear verbatim, as written script in the Holy Bible. However the "idea" of the remnant church is present in numerous places in the Word of God. Although this concept is not included in the dogma of major denominations and non-denominational organizations, the reality of it cannot be understated. As a result of the prevailing escapist mentality in the Body of Christ, the idea of a remnant church is not a popular notion, nor a major teaching. In fact, this idea is rarely presented, if at all, because it intimates that the Church will be in the earth after the great tribulation has taken place. This idea is definitely taboo among most conservative and evangelical Christians. The reality is that most church bodies teach that the saints will be raptured before the great tribulation, or at best, in the middle of it. The concept of the remnant church is actually an affront to most Christians, due to the fact that it contradicts the message being propagated by the popular "Left Behind" series.

However the fact remains that the idea of a remnant Church can be seen throughout the Bible. While it can be argued that the

Old Testament references to "the remnant" are a direct reference to the nation of Israel, we must deal with the mention of that idea in the New Testament.[37] Additionally, attention must be given to the reality that the 1st century New Testament Church also symbolically represents spiritual Israel, and in and of itself can be considered a remnant. It is the remainder or leftover part of the original descendants of Abraham, who were looking for the advent of the Messiah. This is the piece that continued in the hope of His coming, and actually received the fact that He had come. So, the concept of the remnant, a smaller portion left behind after the larger portion has been removed, definitely applies to the 1st century New Testament Church.

After the prominence was removed from Judaism and shifted to Christianity, that new group could properly be referred to as a remnant. Although this group was the original "Church," they were still only what resulted once a portion was subtracted and separated out of the larger body; known as followers of Judaism. This body was comprised of ethnic and non-ethnic Jews.

Although primarily composed of Jewish believers, the number of Gentiles who practiced Judaism, which were added to the Church on the Day of Pentecost, cannot be overlooked. We must remember that the initial group of believers who responded to the gospel message on the Day of Pentecost was ethnic Jews, and non-ethnic persons who practiced Judaism. I believe that the contemporary Body of Christ has severely missed the fact that the majority of the Holy Scriptures were primarily written by Jews for Jews. We often lose sight of the fact that we actually worship Yahweh, the God of the Hebrews, or Jews, and that our Savior is

CHAPTER TWO: WHY A REMNANT CHURCH?

the Jewish Messiah; Yeshua Ha'Mashiach.

Therefore, as we begin our discussion of the Remnant Church, we must start from the perspective of that Church being intrinsically related to the people of Israel. To explore the concept of a remnant, as it pertains to the 1st century New Testament Remnant Church and the modern-day conformist-Church, one must acknowledge her inherent Jewish foundation. There is an inescapable attachment of the Church to Israel. To attempt to ignore this is ludicrous. Too often, the modern-day Church has been guilty of not acknowledging that she worships the God of the Hebrews; the God of the Jews. In times past, she has sometimes tried to act like Christianity has an access to God that precludes in association with Israel. Sometimes she forgot that without the nation of Israel, and God's attachment to her, the Gentile Church would be non-existent. She has been guilty of trying to disassociate her future from the destiny of Israel. She has tried to interpret apocalyptic prophetic scriptures without having the Jewish nation as the central focus of those prophecies. Thanks be to God that He is currently, actively correcting that erroneous presumption on the part of the modern-day Church. He is making it abundantly clear, on many different platforms, that His plan for the end of the age and the Church, cannot come to pass without Israel playing a major part in it.

In times past, many people and ethnic groups have viewed the Jews as enemies of humanity; greedy, selfish, and self-promoting. Anti-Semitism would attempt to have us believe the blessing that is upon these chosen people as something they themselves control. The Jews are the recipients of the blessing of

Jehovah, and will always be the recipient of that blessing. Just as the descendants of Ishmael (the Arabs), Abraham's first born[38] received the inheritance and blessing of the first born, and in spite of their religious error are still a blessed people.[39] Even so, the Jews, in spite of rejecting their Messiah, are still a blessed people. The Church has been fortunate enough to have been grafted into her, and now receives the same covenant blessings and promises reserved for the "seed" of Abraham.[40] Now that she is composed of persons of faith, the Church is also the "seed" of Abraham.[41]

    One cannot speak of the New Testament Church without intentionally correlating her to the root from which she springs, Israel; the Jewish nation. It is impossible to examine eschatological truths without admitting the fundamental Hebrew composition of the Prophets, Apostles, supporting cast, and central figure of this great ensemble of characters. In its birth, as the 1st century Church moved out of Judaism, Jehovah was leading her from the bondage of the Law into the liberty of the Spirit. As I heard Bishop William L. Washington, say in 2000, "Just because you are free doesn't mean you have to be loose." Although the Law bound those Jewish believers, it also kept them until the Messiah was manifested, and could endow them with the power of The Holy Spirit. It is the power of the Holy Ghost that provides the means for living within the context of the Kingdom of God. The Law was intended to point the Jews to the Messiah, while simultaneously showing them that they did not have what it took to observe all 613 statutes of the Law, the Mitzvot. As the early New Testament Church emerged from Judaism, she was to be faced with many perilous times.

CHAPTER TWO: WHY A REMNANT CHURCH?

However, the most perilous time she was about to face was not the long period of persecution. It was the "looseness" she was about to experience as she grew and matured. Quite to the contrary of the persecution she had suffered, it was her acceptance as the state religion of Rome that would prove to be her most perilous time. Her being blended into a system full of sun-worshippers would thrust her headlong into a period of deception and compromise. Throughout the history of Israel, there has always been a remnant. From Genesis through the Revelation of Jesus Christ, given to John the beloved disciple, the concept of the remnant has always been present. It has stood as a monument and memorial to commemorate the fact that there has always been a group that has either gone on to a different place; or has been left behind in the same old place. *There has always been a deposit in the earth that was representative of the pure purpose of God. He has always made sure that there would be a smaller part left after the larger part was gone. His plan and purpose insured that the smaller part would still have the power and capacity to fulfill the mission that had been assigned to the larger part.*

In the Old Testament the "remnant" represented God's chosen people, the Jews. Abraham and his descendants were the smaller group that remained after God separated the human race at the Tower of Babel. As mankind built a tower into the heavens, to escape another flooding of the earth should God have decided to send one, they began to try to govern in an area where God had not given them jurisdiction. The command to Adam was, *"be fruitful, multiply, replenish the earth, subdue it, and have dominion over it."*[42] Nowhere in that command is there any mention of having dominion over the heavens. They were seeking to establish themselves in an area that was reserved for spiritual dominance. So, out of the whole of all the inhabitants on the earth at that time, God separated one man, and gave that man exclusive access to Himself.

Prior to the Tower of Babel, the whole of creation had access to Jehovah. He had made Himself available to anyone who would seek him. He was an all-inclusive God; no particular group of people could claim sole ownership or access to Him. He was a God of everyone, and for everyone. After the Tower of Babel, Jehovah became the God of the Hebrews. After He confused the languages, He separated Himself a remnant out of that mass of confusion, Abram, and made Himself exclusively available to Abram and his descendants. That remnant became the portion of creation that would be responsible for nurturing a relationship with the living God, and housing the bloodline that would bring forth the Savior for the whole world. That small group of people would ultimately be responsible for saving the whole of creation. That remnant would maintain a right relationship with God, while the rest of the world would fall victim to the god of this world; who deceived its inhabitants with the "I, Me, My Syndrome." Israel would be the remnant that would not conform or be seduced into the deceptive ways of "the kingdom of self," invariably known as the kingdom of darkness.

In the New Testament the "remnant" represented God's chosen people, comprised of the Jewish and Gentile (non-Jewish) believers who have accepted Jehovah's Messiah, Jesus of Nazareth, as the Christ of God. It is interesting to note, and one should pay close attention to the fact that I am always referring to the remnant as, "God's chosen people." We must be mindful of the fact that remnant always exists by election or selection. The remnant does not "will" itself into existence, but rather exists at the pleasure and by the will of the Father. The Remnant Church does not accidentally come forth, trip into purpose, or stumble into destiny. The Remnant Church is a deliberate, ordained, selected group of people. They have a pre-ordained purpose, a pre-planned course of action, and a predestined destination. They exist as an extension of God's continual plan to perfect the Church, and insure that she lives up to His original purpose for her. God has always been in search of a people who would voluntarily serve Him, obey His command, and seek to do His will. He has always been pursuing the remnant; a people with a passion for serving God's agenda.

So, after God demonstrated to man that mankind was incapable of maintaining innocence, living by conscience, being constrained by human government, or keeping the law; He had to make another intervention. He had to initiate a time of grace, where He would extend mercy to sinful man; by the sacrifice of His dear son, Jesus of Nazareth. Virgin born Jesus, who fulfilled prophecy, lived a sinless life, died a substitutionary death, was raised from the dead after three days, and now calls men everywhere to repent. When the ethnic Jews and the non-ethnic Jews who practiced Judaism realized that they could not keep the Law as a means of maintaining relationship with Jehovah; they submitted to God's plan for them to become a remnant. As they received the message of salvation on the Day of Pentecost, and responded with a repentant acceptance of the Messiah, a remnant was birthed. The 1st century New Testament Remnant Church, those Jewish Disciples of Christ and the three thousand added on the Day of Pentecost, emerged out of the exclusive religion of Judaism, and the Creator was once again inclusively available to all of creation.

> *"In the New Testament the 'remnant' represented God's chosen people, comprised of the Jewish and Gentile (non-Jewish) believers who have accepted Jehovah's Messiah, Jesus of Nazareth, as the Christ of God."*

Whether Old Covenant or New Covenant, there has always been a remnant associated with the Hebrew people, and there will always be a remnant associated with the Jewish nation. The idea of a remnant is necessary as a way of God preserving the purity of His intentions, and the accomplishment of His purpose. Despite the constant attempts, and success, of the enemy to pollute what God has intended to be a reflection of His holiness; there will always be a portion of the original group that refuses to bow down, refuses to compromise, and refuses to accept the deception, the remnant. Throughout the history of God dealing with His people, He has always made provision for an elected portion of the whole to remain true to the call, true to the vision, true to the mission of accomplishing His purpose, the remnant. In His foreknowledge, God is acutely aware of the fact that leaven will seep in to try to sidetrack His purpose, defeat His ultimate strategy of redeeming the world to Himself, and perpetrate the deception of satan upon the creation. Jehovah selects a people, and makes the option of non-compromise available to them. Some choose that option, while others choose the compromise. In any event, there is always a group that will

CHAPTER TWO: WHY A REMNANT CHURCH?

stay on task; a group that will not give in; a group that will stay the course, the remnant.

God's Word, which proceeds out of His mouth, will not return unto Him void. It will prosper, and accomplish the purpose whereunto it has been sent. In order for this foundational truth to remain constant, there must be a way to circumvent the enemy's attack on this vital truth. This truth is central to the Christian's ability to take God at His Word. It is at the core of the believer's ability to have unconditional confidence and trust in the Word they have heard from God; which is what faith is. It is the essential component, and platform, upon which the Church is built; for if the Word of God is not able to perform what He promises; then God is a liar, and cannot be trusted. In order to safeguard His Word, and guarantee the manifestation of everything He has spoken, God has put a stop-gap in place. There is an instrument that will insure the fulfillment of His Word, His intentions, and His purpose, the remnant.

God is a covenant giving God, and a covenant keeping God. Covenant is the context in which God has extended relationship to His people. Blood covenant, in particular, is the mandatory context in which man must relate to his God, Jehovah, the Ancient of Days, the Great I Am; the God of the Hebrews. It is the thing that made Able's sacrifice superior to Cain's; sacrifice; it is what made Able's sacrifice acceptable. It is steeped in the notion of obedience. Without the shedding of blood, there is no forgiveness of sin.[43] Blood covenant is a mutual and binding agreement between two or more parties, and is made at the incision where the blood flows. It reflects the nature of our relationship with the Creator, and is overshadowed with the concept of reciprocity. There are certain provisions that must be kept, certain terms of covenant that must be maintained in order for the Church to receive what God has promised her. Some of the promises of God are unconditional, other sare definitely conditional. We call these "conditional promises" "terms of covenant." God has positioned the provision of "the remnant" in place to insure that the terms of covenant are kept, thereby providing Him the ability to keep His Word, and bring to fruition the promises He has made to His people.

God honors His Word above His name, He will go to great lengths to make sure that His Word is kept, and His promises are delivered.

"I will worship toward thy holy temple, and praise thy name for thy lovingkindness and for thy truth; for thou hast magnified thy word above all thy name" Psalm 138:2

The Remnant Church is a means of God ensuring that the purity of His intentions and Word are actualized. So, throughout the Old and New Covenants He has made sure that there was, and will be, a remnant to remain true to the expressed purpose that has proceeded out of His heart, mouth, and mind. Therefore, in the Old and New Testaments of the Bible, you will always find the concept of "the remnant."

Since the Old Covenant is the covenant that God made with Abram and his descendants; it is God's covenant with the Hebrew, or Jewish nation. Since the New Covenant is the covenant God made with those who accepted the Messiah sent to the Jews; it is God's covenant with the Messianic Hebrew or Jewish nation, and all that have been grafted into her; the Gentile Church, the "seed" of Abraham.[44] The question is not so much whether we recognize, or accept, the impending existence of The Remnant Church, as much as it is do we recognize the significance of The Remnant Church.

Whether or not we recognize the existence of this Church does not invalidate her being; or discourage God from causing her to emerge. God will not allow anything or anyone to prevent His purpose from being accomplished. He will be undaunted by the world's refusal to recognize the provision He has established; to allow all of His prophetic Word to be fulfilled. He is impervious to our unbelief; or lack of acceptance of the notion of a Remnant Church. He understands that there must be a body of believers in place, who are not influenced by this world system; a group of people who will not buy into the compromise. He knows that if there is to be a group of believers who are not deceived by the enemy's allurement to be socially and politically correct; there has to be a Remnant Church. There has to be a Church that will maintain the principles of, "touch not the unclean thing..., come out from among her, and be ye separate..." Even though as a "labeled" entity, she may not appear in Scripture; as a concept, she is clearly visible, and has never been hidden. He also knows that the emergence of the Remnant Church is paramount to dispelling the idea that He is okay with compromise, and is in agreement with a Church that will not stand her ground on the extreme issues. He has no pleasure in a Church that is looking to establish herself in the middle of the controversial issues; a Church that would rather be non-offensive than be one which causes polarization.[45]

As was stated previously, there are a couple concepts that are not literally mentioned in the Scriptures, yet they are fundamental truths upon which many people's faith is built. If you look for these words in the Bible, you will not find them. Yet the reality of what they represent is inescapable, and is a much valued tenet in the Christian belief system of many people. Words such as rapture and trinity cannot be found on the written page, but are concepts printed in the hearts and minds of many believers. Additionally, they are concepts clearly defined, and represented on the written pages of the Bible. So too is the concept of The Remnant Church. It is much like the example that Jesus used with Nicodemus; as He explained the wind.

"The wind bloweth where it listeth, and thou heareth the sound thereof, and cannot tell whence it cometh, and whither it goest: so is everyone who is born of the Spirit." John. 3:8

While you cannot literally see the wind, its affects are unmistakable. So, it is with the Remnant Church, even though we don't see her literally mentioned on the written page; her impending emergence and cataclysmic impact are undeniable. God doesn't break His pattern; He changes not. He will always allow that portion to remain, which will accomplish His purpose.

What is the significance of the Remnant Church?

CHAPTER TWO: WHY A REMNANT CHURCH?

> What is her importance, meaning, and worth?
>
> What is the implication of having a Remnant Church in the earth?
>
> What is the consequence and impact of having this body of believers around the world?

If we compare this end-times Remnant Church to the 1st century New Testament Remnant Church, the significance is earth changing, and has implications that will disrupt life in the highest places of government. If the end-times Remnant Church is a time-span parallel of her former self, then the world needs to be prepared to be turned upside down. As it was in the beginning, so shall it be at the end. It is safe to say that the latter shall be greater than the former.[46]

There are some Scriptures that are specifically written to ethnic Jewish people. There is no way that we can dispute this fact. The thing we need to begin to understand is that as the Church, we have been grafted into that primarily Jewish body. How dare we forget that the majority of the crowd who heard the Pentecost message was Jewish? The Church started with the Jews, and will end with the Jews. The time is fast approaching when all of Israel will be saved. Their blessings are our blessings; their curses are our curses. We have become a part of them; in totality. Our destiny is linked to them; so that wherever they go, so goes the Church. We are simply amazed that theologians want to separate the prophetic promises made to Israel from the prophetic promises made to the Church. The Church has no promises save the ones that are associated with Israel. The Church can ill-afford to let

Replacement Theology cause her to think that there is one set of promises for Jews, and another set of promises for Gentiles. There are only promises for believers and promises for non-believers. Promises for the faithful, (Abraham's seed) and promises for the faithless. There are provisions for the Body of Christ, which is one body, and lack of provision for those belonging to the kingdom of darkness. There is neither Jew nor Gentile, bond nor free, male nor female; all are one in Christ Jesus.

> *"Words such as rapture and trinity cannot be found on the written page, but are concepts printed in the hearts and minds of many believers."*

"There is neither Jew nor Greek, there is neither bond or free, there is neither male or female: for ye all are one in Christ Jesus." Galatians 3:28

We must bear in mind the simple fact that the end-times Remnant Church, which reflects the power, authority, and nature of her 1st century counterpart, will be the vehicle that sparks Israel to jealousy. She will be the vessel that reminds the Jews that salvation was to the Jew first, and then to the Gentiles. [47]The Remnant Church will provide the spark that causes the light to come on for the nation of Israel. She will be the catalyst that prompts the Jews to finally understand that Christianity is the grown up child of Judaism. Israel will ultimately accept that Christianity is the result of the whole world recognizing Jehovah, the God of the Hebrews, as the one and only true living God. They will be prompted by the end-times Remnant Church to finally see that Jesus of Nazareth, whom they crucified, is in fact

CHAPTER TWO: WHY A REMNANT CHURCH?

the Jewish Messiah that the nation of Israel was waiting for. The Remnant Church will be responsible for ushering in the great end-time harvest of Jewish converts to Christ. This cataclysmic event alone will change the course of human history. Our finite mind cannot begin to fathom the impact this change of religious position will have upon human government. The ripple effect that this will have on the course of mankind is mind-boggling. The world will truly be turned upside down; just as it was in the days of the 1st century Church. There will be major realignments of world governments. The Islamic holy jihad will have new fuel for its fire. The hatred of the alliance between the United States and Israel will heighten to levels not even imaginable. The stage will be set for the greatest war of all times. The appearance of The Remnant Church will also signal a drastic intensification in the level of spiritual warfare conducted by the Body of Christ.

The compromised, deceived, conformist-Church will no longer be in a position of power to block the move of the Holy Ghost in the earthly body of believers; those empowered to be God's delegated authority and designated representative in the earth. The remnant will be an agent in the earth duly authorized to do battle against the kingdom of darkness, and intent on doing just that. A cadre of Servant Warriors dedicated to function in the same manner as their Commander in Chief, Jesus; the author and finisher of our faith.

"Looking unto Jesus the author and finisher of our faith; who for the joy that was set before Him endured the cross, despising the shame, and is set down at the right hand of the throne of God." Hebrews 12:2

An army of believers equipped to wage war against the darkness; with a sworn commitment to destroy the works of the enemy.

"He that committeth sin is of the devil; for the devil sinneth from the beginning. For this purpose the son of God was manifested, that He might destroy the works of the devil." I John 3:8

The emergence of the end-times Remnant Church represents a return to the fiery vigor and vitality that was present as the Holy Spirit of God made Himself available to dwell in the physical earthen bodies of as many as would receive Him. She represents a well-oiled, fighting machine, with a single driven focus to wreak havoc upon her archenemy; satan, the imps of hell, and the kingdom of darkness.

The word remnant is also usually associated with the idea of a portion that is left over. We commonly label "leftovers" as things that are not as good as the principals that served as their original source. They are typically seen with a negative connotation. Leftovers are commonly viewed as something less desirable than the main course; from which they are the remainder. They are usually served in an attempt to clean out the refrigerator, or rid the shelves of excess; in preparation to receive a new shipment. They are often sold at a discount price, due to their lack of size or perceived inability to fill a significant space in a large room. It signifies something that remains after the rest of the whole has been depleted, exhausted or otherwise used up. In other words, remnants are perceived as that which remains after the best part has been utilized, and the finest resources have been drawn upon. Stated another way, the remnant is construed to be that which is left over when the preeminent assets have been brought into play, and applied to the situation. It has inherent in its definition, the idea of not being complete; or in some way being deficient. Leftovers are deemed not to be complete, full, or comprehensive. They are usually associated with not being ample. Likewise, the remnant is all too often perceived as being scarce, lacking, underprovided, undersupplied, and wanting. It is not typically related to the notion of completeness, nor is it normally perceived as a positive attribute.

None of the worldly attributes mentioned above apply to the remnant of our discussion. The Remnant Church that emerges at the end of the age is the antithesis of all the things alluded to in our discussion of "leftovers." In fact, the remnant is the exact opposite of these things, and stands in direct contrast to the images envisioned when we speak of leftovers. She represents the preeminent resources; this is why she has been called forth. She has what the compromised, deceived, conformist-Church is lacking. The Remnant Church has the provision. She has the supply, and an abundance of it. She is complete, and full of the power of God. She is totally comprehensive, and capable of fulfilling the divine purpose for which the Church was established. She IS the best part of the Church, and is the finest resource that God has to offer this sin-sick generation. The remnant is ample; as a matter of fact she is more than enough. If enough is that which satisfies, she is more than satisfaction; she is fulfillment. The Remnant Church is not lacking in size, or ability to fill the void that has been created by the deceived, conformist-Church. The remnant is abounding in the flavor of God, and has the ability to preserve the world in the midst of the onslaught of evil; that will be experienced as this present darkness intensifies.

As we explore the remnant in the Old Testament, we do it from the perspective of understanding that the remnant is the part of something that is left when other parts are gone. It is something smaller being used to fulfil that which the larger part failed to accomplish. It reinforces the idea that something which is void of its other parts, parts which appeared to be necessary, is still able to function in the purpose and role for which it was created, and intended to be used.

If we start with the lineage of the children of Adam and Eve, we can see the principle of the remnant in operation. We find a situation that begins with an account of all of Adam and Eve's children; even though there were only two initially listed. After the death of Able, we are informed of the other descendants of this couple; however, only the descendants of Seth receive a detailed accounting and description throughout the rest of the Scriptures. Once again, we note the operation of the remnant in place. Although Adam lived to be nine hundred and thirty years old, and had numerous descendants, the Bible only deals with the remnant of Seth's lineage; those who had been elected to be the bloodline through which Messiah Jesus would be born.[48]

Look again and you will see the concept of the remnant in the account of Noah and the flood.[49] It is painstakingly obvious that this man and his family were separated from the entire human race, and chosen to be the means by which Jehovah would repopulate the earth after He totally destroyed it. What a heavy responsibility was on Noah and his family. They were tasked with the regeneration of the entire world. Theirs was the responsibility to restore and rejuvenate a planet that had experienced a death sentence more severe than the one which was imposed on Pharaoh and the Egyptians. It was an angel of death sent to the first born that would influence the Egyptians to release God's chosen people from the bondage of slavery; in their land of captivity.[50] Yet, Jehovah believed that Noah and his family, the remnant, had the desirable quality it would take to bring life out of the devastation of the death of the entire human race caused by the great flood.

The nation of Israel was continually finding herself in a position where she was in some way operating in the role of a remnant. She was notorious for experiencing the pruning process of God. Let us begin with the call of faithful Abram. We will notice a pattern prevalent in earlier encounters of mankind with his Creator; which we will take a closer examination of its continued use. Abram was called out from among the totality of the then known world, separated from known civilization, and asked to do the unthinkable. He was asked to leave his familiar surroundings, go to an unknown place, to serve an angry God who had just thrown the whole of humanity into a tailspin. He was singled out, removed from a place of safety, and cast into a journey with an unknown destination, with only the promise of greatness; from a God who had just exacted a horrific judgment on His disobedient creation. Do you think that Abram was going to tell Him no? He was being asked to do what the whole of humanity had just failed to do; obediently serve God, and govern in the sphere where they were designated to have authority. He was being asked to accomplish this without the support systems he was accustomed to, and he was expected to succeed in doing so.

As we look at the concept of The Remnant Church, we must do so with the realization that it is a deliberate function that God allows; so that His purpose can be accomplished. In the world of the Spirit, there is no such thing as an accidental remnant. The remnant is intentionally elected by God to fulfill what the group, out of which it has been extracted, could not fulfill. When we study the situation surrounding Isaac and Ishmael, we see another example of parts not destroyed or used up. These boys were chosen to stay in place and be unchanged; even though their parents got in the way and tried to help God out. Abraham and Sarah mistakenly thought that God needed their assistance to fulfill His prophetic promise concerning them. Yet in spite of their mistake, God chose to bless both sons with descendants who would frame the course of world history; then and now. Ishmael's twelve sons would go on to produce the Arab nations; which certainly have impacted world events. While the descendants of Isaac, the child of promise, would produce the twelve tribes of Israel; who also have certainly impacted world history. Neither of these world changers have been able to be destroyed or used; even though there have been multiple attempts against each group to do exactly that. They remain the remnant elected by grace and mercy.

Jacob and Esau also represent the concept of the remnant. What we see is the one to whom the prophetic promise was spoken having to separate himself from the larger group in order to function in the role and capacity that had been reserved for

Abraham. The reality is that everyone who has ever received God's free gift of salvation is the beneficiary of the promise God made to Abraham; that all nations/families of the earth would be blessed in him.

> *"And I will bless them that bless thee, and curse them that curseth thee: and in thee shall all families of the earth be blessed."* Genesis 12:3

The nation of Israel, the Hebrew descendants of Abraham, strayed from the God of their forefathers. They were in danger of being cast aside from receiving the benefits and provisions of the covenants of promise. Had it not been for the promise God made to Abraham and David, there would be no hope for the Jews; or mankind. The conditions of covenant mandated obedience to the commands, and worship of God; relative to the terms of covenant. When Israel went whoring after other gods, she violated the terms of the covenant. By rights, Jehovah was no longer obligated to fulfill His part of the agreement; because Israel had failed to keep her part. The saving grace for Israel, and the world, was that God had foreknowledge of the dilemma in which mankind would find itself, so He purposed to extract a remnant out of those disobedient Jews. He had to have a group separated from those idol worshippers; in order to keep the Davidic bloodline open and available for usage.

Purposing to have a group left over, that would still be determined to maintain relational purity with Yahweh, was the only way He could send the Messiah through the descendants of Abraham and David. If there were not a remnant during the time of the divided kingdom, it would have been impossible for the seed of David to fulfill her prophetic destiny. The only way God could remain true to His Word to send a Savior, and defeat the enemy, was for a remnant to remain which would be committed to the purpose for which God had originally established His chosen people.

God made a promise to crush the enemy's head, back in the Garden of Eden, which could only be fulfilled by there being a remnant of David's seed, Jesse's seed, Abraham's seed, Seth's seed, and Adam's seed. The whole idea of a remnant being in place was the only way Israel could achieve God's expectation of her to be the vessel through which He could redeem His lost creation. Not only was remnant theology significant to Israel then, but it is also significant now. Paul's discourse on the remnant in the 9th through 11th chapters of the book of Romans allows us to understand that the hope for all of Israel's salvation is predicated upon there being a remnant in place. There must be a leftover remainder to encourage the Jews to accept the Christ of God; who happens to be Jesus of Nazareth, Yeshua Ha'Mashiach.

The spiritual Gentiles are the recipients of God's mercy and grace, having been grafted into the provisions made for natural Israel. It is of paramount importance for the spiritual Gentiles to understand the role they play in relationship to Israel and her remnant. The Church must acknowledge that salvation is first and foremost of, and for, the Jew. The Holy Scriptures were written by, and for, Jews. God, in His omniscience, knew that the Jews would not receive Jesus as their Messiah. Their rejection of Him paved the way for the Gentiles to be saved. However, The Church must never get it twisted, and think that Jehovah has given up on the Jewish nation. The Church must never delude herself into thinking that God has abandoned Israel for His "new chosen people." She can ill-afford to adopt that philosophy, for to do so will invalidate all the New Covenant promises; which, in fact, were made to the Jews.

The Gentile Church is a tool that God will use to draw a remnant out from among the Jewish nation. This Jewish remnant, which is drawn to Christianity, will be instrumental in drawing the whole of Israel to salvation.[58] The Gentile Church will be used by God to make the Jews jealous. She will bring them to the realization that Christians are experiencing, and are in possession of, the salvation that was originally intended for God's chosen people; the Jews. As she ministers here at the end of the age, the Remnant Church that will emerge out of the compromised, deceived, conformist-Church must bear in mind that her function is to serve as the catalyst that makes the Jews jealous enough to want the brand of worship they see being given to their God, the Ancient of Days...Jehovah. In order to make them jealous, The Remnant Church cannot be guilty of offering up "strange fire."[59] Her worship and lifestyle must be exemplary and beyond reproach; it must be pure. She has to be walking the life she is talking about. Holiness must not be something the Jews have to search to find in The Remnant Church, but rather should be the apparel in which the remnant is clothed. The Remnant Church will have to appear as an organism without spot or blemish, to attract a group of people who are intent upon keeping all of the Law as the means of having relationship with Jehovah. There has to be a holy remnant to spark the Jews to receive the Messiah, and thereby fulfill their destiny.

As we examine the Book of Acts, we can explore and discover the makeup of the original New Testament Church. First and foremost, we must recognize that the event at which the Church was birthed was one of the major traditional festivals of the Jews. The Feast of Pentecost was celebrated seven weeks after the end of the Feast of Passover. The Jews had been celebrating Passover since 1300 B.C. It was a traditional celebration of the Jews, by the Jews, for the Jews, and for those of other ethnicities; who had been converted to the practice of Judaism. So, just as the original recipients of salvation were Jewish,[60] so were the initial recipients of the Holy Ghost on "Resurrection Day" primarily Jewish,[61] and the vast majority of those who were birthed into the Church on the Day of Pentecost were ethnic Jews. Along with Christ's disciples, these converts on the Day of Pentecost could properly be referred to as the first "Messianic Jews."

In addition to these Jewish converts to Christianity, there were also non-ethnic practitioners of Judaism who converted to Christianity on that day. There were people from Mesopotamia, Judea, Cappadocia, Asia, Phrygia, Pamphylia, Egypt, Libya, Italy, and Arabia [62] who became members of the 1st century remnant New Testament Church that day. So, that in what has been termed the birth of the New Testament Church, we can see the prophecy Jehovah made to father Abraham, of being a blessing to the whole world, beginning to be fulfilled. It would take quite a while for all nations to be blessed through him and his seed. Nevertheless, the emergence of an inclusive Church, out of a religion that for over two thousand years had been exclusive to the Jews, was an indicator the promises of God to faithful Abraham were coming to fruition.

As we read further in Acts, we will find Paul, an aggressive evangelist, reaching out to the other Gentile inhabitants who were not practicing Judaism. We can see the advance of the Gospel message being made among people who were not present at the Feast of Pentecost. We can see attempts being made to convert people who were actively worshipping idols and false gods. We can see the borders of the 1st century New Testament Church expanding across the boundaries of the nation of Israel, and extending to the farthest reaches of the Roman Empire. Neither Jew nor Gentile, bond nor free, neither male nor female, but an inclusive worldwide aggregation of believers and worshippers of the God of the Hebrews, and His Jewish Messiah; the 1st century remnant New Testament Church was alive and well.

A major shift happened for the early Church as a result of Constantine's vision, victory and subsequent declaration of his Christianity. That shift involved a basic change in the apostolic leadership and governance of the Church. It also reflected a change in the requisites necessary to become a member of the Body of Christ, and receive the benefits of the free gift of salvation. This shift also helped to eliminate the virtue and sacrificial lifestyle which had come into place with the emergence of the 1st century New Testament Remnant Church; as it emerged out of the shadows of Judaism. The Remnant Church that surfaced on the Day of Pentecost was earmarked by acts of repentance, which resulted in a sacrifice of self-pleasing behavior; in exchange for living a life that was submitted to the priority of pleasing God. As Constantine's actions gave way to a new brand of Christianity that was void of the concept of repentance, we can see one of the first vestiges of compromise and deception seeping into this newly formed remnant.

Repentance was the message of John the Baptist, Jesus, and the apostolic leaders of the 1st century Church. It is a concept that had been espoused by Jehovah, through the prophets, all throughout the Old Testament. It is a necessary "turn" that has to take place in order to begin walking in the right direction. Before one can properly follow God, they first have to turn from going the wrong way, in their own direction, and get pointed in the right direction; this is what repentance is. With the advent of Rome's new Christianity that proposed one could be born or baptized into a relationship with the Church, a deception was being birthed, and a seduction was being enabled. If there were no need to repent and change what one is doing, who wouldn't want to be Christian. This marked the beginnings of a lowering of the standards which had been put in place by the Christ, and His apostles. This began to remove the criteria of a changed life to be the distinction by which those who belonged to "the way" could be recognized. The relaxing of these standards resulted in a form of worship that was more of a ritual, than one of a lifestyle that reflected a personal relationship with God.

Ultimately, Constantine's personal deception was advanced from being an edict of toleration to being a government mandated requirement in order for citizens to conduct business in the Roman Empire. What had started out being a voluntary decision to accept God's provision and His answer to the sin question had been transformed into a mandatory government regulation and law. What a deception, what a compromise, what a seduction. What a tragedy had befallen this newly formed 1st century New Testament Remnant Church. With this compromise we see the origins of the Holy Roman Catholic Church, and the basis and opportunity for the establishment of the Eastern Orthodox Church. These were the early deceived, conformist-Churches from which the Protestant Reformation, the mid-century Remnant Church, would emerge.

As we further explore the 1st century – 4th century New Testament Remnant Church, it is interesting to note that by the end of the 1st century there were only 1,000 Jewish Christians left in the Roman Empire.[63] Some Hebrew Christians sought refuge from persecution in the city of Maximianopolis on the plains of Megiddo, while others sought refuge in the city of Pella in the country of Jordan. Still others sought sanctuary in other cities in the Decapolis. These cities included: Gerasa (Jerash); Scyhthopolis (Beit She'an); Hippos; Gadara (Umm Qais); Pella; Philadelphia (Amman); Capitolias (Dion); Canatha (Qanawat); Raphana (Abila), and Damascus. More sought refuge in the Qumran communities and in Arabia.[64] These Judeo Christian communities were groups labeled as Ebionites, Judaizers, and Nazarenes, and represented communities in which traditional Jewish worship and form were practiced. Additionally, there were other cities where Jewish form or Jewish worship was incorporated into the new Christian way

> *"This shift also helped to eliminate the virtue and sacrificial lifestyle which had come into place..."*

of life; with acceptance of Jesus of Nazareth as Jehovah's Messiah. These people were known as Bereans, Bashanitis, and Pasagians.

According to Church history, as relayed by Eusebius, there were Jewish Christian Bishops until the Bar Kokhba Revolt in or about 132-136 A.D.[65] Post Constantine, there were also Jewish Christian communities in Egypt, India, Syria, Lebanon, and Greece.[66] These communities, which did not succumb to the practices of the Holy Roman Catholic and Eastern Orthodox Church, resulted in and contributed to the formation of the Syriac Orthodox Church, Greek Orthodox Church, and Melkite Greek Catholic Church.[67] In spite of the effect of the Roman Empire stealing the governance of the Church from the hands of the Jewish apostles, there was still a Jewish influence on the practices of Christianity after the Constantine era. There was still a remnant that practiced the form in which the Church had been birthed at Pentecost. There was then, and always will be a Remnant Church.

When Jesus returns, He will be looking for a Church that resembles the one He deposited in the earth when He left. He will be searching for a body that is without spot or blemish, like the one that was fashioned when He came back in the form of the Holy Ghost, on the Day of Pentecost,

> *"That He might present it to Himself a glorious church, not having spot or wrinkle, or any such thing; but that it should be holy and without blemish."*
> Ephesians 5:27

He came back to indwell those who would dare to come out from among the old dead way of keeping the Law (Judaism).

CHAPTER TWO: WHY A REMNANT CHURCH?

The 1st century New Testament Remnant Church was called to come into a relationship with God, through Jesus Christ. In this relationship, the God of creation would be allowed to inhabit His new temple, the bodies of the "called out ones."

"What? know ye not that your body is the temple of the Holy Ghost which is in you, which ye have of God, and ye are not your own." I Corinthians 6:19

Our returning Savior will be in search of a Church that is walking in the power and authority that replicates that of the Church birthed on Pentecost; a Church standing as the personification of the power for which it stands in proxy. The Lion of the tribe of Judah will be looking for that body of believers who are casting out demons and defying natural science; by the working of the power of God in them.

He will be in quest of those who have given all things in common, and are committed to evangelization of their own world as a daily lifestyle.

He will be seeking those in the earth who are the quintessence of the propagation of the principles of the Kingdom of God.

He will be looking for those who are accurately representing His image in the earth.

He will be seeking those who are an active part of the proliferation of the spiritual message of no compromise, no conformity, no surrender to seducing spirits of religion.

He will be looking for The Remnant Church.

"And we know that all things work together for good to them that love God, to them who are the called according to his purpose." Romans 8:28

Chapter Three

The Sum Total & The Remnant

Looking at The Remnant Church, it is easy to classify her as the sum total of all things, recognizing what she represents. As far as accomplishing God's intended purpose of the Church, *driving the Jewish nation to salvation;* the reality of her completeness is an inescapable fact. Though she might only be that which is left over, she yet remains full of all of the virtue and power necessary to stand as a bulwark and tower against the pressing forces of darkness. This is true in spite of the massive falling away from the principles upon which the 1st century Church was founded. She may be small in her personage and number, yet she still possesses every milligram of anointing needed to break the yokes of bondage, and set the captives free. Her commitment to fulfilling purpose causes her stature and greatness to loom as a formidable foe against the hordes of satan. She stands unwavering against the deceptive winds of doctrine, as they try to blow her into the sea of compromise. Yet, she stands like the proud palm tree with her roots going deep and anchoring around that immovable stone; so as not to break under the winds of false doctrine. Instead, she sways, bends, and seems so vulnerable. Yet, her purpose and destiny are anchored in the set gift, who Himself is the Chief Apostle, Chief Prophet, Chief Evangelist, Chief Pastor and Chief Teacher—Jesus, the Christ of God.

Nothing can sway the end-times Remnant Church from walking the plumb line, as she ministers in power and authority. She is the culmination of everything the Father intended the visible Body of Christ to be in the earth; His emissary and manifested representation in the earth. She literally sums up all that God wants to do in the earth; to bring all of His prophetic promises to pass.

A sum is a total arrived at through the counting of all involved parts. It is the total accounting of everything that has been put into the formula as a component necessary to cause the whole to function. The Remnant Church represents the totality of all that God purposed for His called-out ones. She is the aggregate of what He expects the Church to look like, and function like. She is the full summation of God's design against the enemy, and the kingdom of darkness. She is the whole and total completeness of Jehovah's strategy to have a body that will function in similarity to the One sent out of eternity to destroy the works of the devil.

The Remnant Church is the overall comprehensiveness of the Father's intention to punish evil, and execute judgment against those who willfully disobey His commands, and refuse to accept His Messiah. She stands as the amassing, and lion's share, of the weaponry He has designated to decimate the forces of seduction and deception. She stands opposed to the great liar that has aligned against the masses of humanity; as mankind seeks to come into true relationship with the only true and living God. The end-times Remnant Church is the entirety of the volume of the "moves of God," in this sphere known as time; as He prepares to usher the world into eternity. She is the manifestation of the anointing of God in human flesh. She serves as an extension of the ministry of Christ in the earth.

The remnant is the weapon which the Father is prepared to utilize against the god of this world; as Jehovah finishes the war that was started in Heaven when He had to kick lucifer out. The Remnant Church represents the entire total volume of truth and the combined cumulative amount of restorative purity, needed to bring about God's salvation to the whole of Israel. She also serves to extend God's provision of salvation to as many Gentiles who will receive His solution to the sin problem, Jesus Christ, Yeshua Ha'Mashiach.

A sum total is the whole amount of its collective parts.

It is a combined group of factors that cooperatively are joined together, and shared in order to function as a whole unit.

It is an aggregate; an amassed collection that is united, cohesive, and unified.

It is a cumulative integration of all of the inclusive factors, resulting in a comprehensive, complete collective; consisting of a summary of the chief points of the otherwise disjointed collection.

It is a full high point representing the greatest maximum outcome, relative to the small parts comprised in the makeup of the spectrum of entities or integers. The sum total speaks to the apex or peak of something.

It is the zenith or highest point possible to be achieved.

It is the pinnacle or capstone; the crescendo or climax.

    The sum total is the crown, the conclusion or finale. The total is the summit, the culmination, the finishing touch. Such is the Remnant Church; she is the culmination of God's plan through the ages. She is the finishing touch to all that He has destined for mankind in general, and for the Hebrew Jewish nation in particular. The end-times Remnant Church is the crescendo; the conclusion of the matter. She is the finale, the last act of God to redeem His creation; she is His crowning touch. She is the sum total of all things. The Remnant Church is the full summation of God's redemptive act to rescue His creation from a penalty He never intended for her to have to experience. All that God has attempted to do, to save His people from a devil's hell, is comprehensively aggregated in the end-times body of believers known as The Remnant Church.

First and foremost, we have to say that the Church is the sum total of God's plan for His people. She epitomizes the Father's plan to culminate His judgment against evil disobedience to His will, His command, and His government, by having a people that would be separated unto Himself. The Church is His crown and glory. She is a trophy with which He can taunt satan. She is the proof that there are human beings who are willing to let Him sit on the throne of their lives; as they live a life that is submitted to His dictates, and governance. The Church is the comprehensive summation of Jehovah's intention of having His creation share eternal life with Him. She is the sum total of His plan for mankind to be eternally in communion with Him. She displays His intention for communion with His creation, as was evidenced by His placement of the Tree of Life in the Garden of Eden.

The Church is the pinnacle of His love for His creation; which can be seen in that the purchase price of her redemption cost Him heaven's best; His Son. The Church exemplifies His willingness to allow a portion of Himself to leave His heavenly existence, house Himself in human flesh, and die a brutal death. He did all of this in order for man to be reunited with Him. This was a part of the "process" necessary to provide the regeneration of man's dead spirit. The "process" is called being "saved" or "born again." God allowed a portion of Himself to be separated from Himself. He left His home in glory, shrouded His divinity with our humanity; yet never lost His divine nature. Jesus allowed Himself to become the sacrificial lamb; in order to satisfy the requirement of there being a shedding of blood for the remission of sin; thereby mediating the New Covenant.

> *"What the blood of bulls and goats sprinkled could not accomplish caused Him to show His great love for mankind."*

The Church, God's dwelling place for those who receive Messiah Jesus, is the prime example of the height of God's good intentions for His creation. Jehovah allowed something that had never happened in all of eternity to take place; in order to restore His creation to the fellowship they had with Him before the fall of Adam. The Father allowed Himself to be separated from the Son for the first time in all of eternity. Not only did the Son leave His heavenly existence to come to earth to die for the "sin" of the world, but He also experienced a disconnection from the Father. Jesus hung on Calvary's cross, to pay the "sin debt" for all of creation; past, present, and future. The Father turned His back upon Him; for God could not look on Jesus as He bore the sin of all humanity. This is what caused Jesus to cry out, "My God, My God, why hast thou forsaken me?" The great price that the Father was willing to pay for the salvation of the world is a manifestation of the finale, and finishing touch, He needed as a statement to verify that the head of the serpent had indeed been crushed.

Whether it is The Remnant Church, the Structural Church, the compromised deceived conformist-Church, or however you

CHAPTER THREE: THE SUM TOTAL & THE REMNANT

want to name it; God has always been searching for a people who would willingly be called out from among the sensual ways of the world to holiness. He always looks for a people willing to operate in a distinct way of serving a holy God. Since the proclamation in the Garden of Eden of a Messiah coming forth to bruise the head of the serpent, God has always had it in His heart to have a people that would be willing to please Him; instead of pleasing themselves. The Church is the sum total of all that God had ever designed for mankind; an eternal existence and relationship between the Creator and His creation.

The Church is the sum total of God's original intention for mankind as He intended for Adam to be His designated authority and delegated representative in the earth. As we look at the Church, and the final instructions she received from Jesus as He went to the Father and prepared to return in the form of the Holy Ghost, we can see that His expectation for her was the same expectation the Father had for Adam. We can hear Him say, "If you love me, obey my commandments." Jesus plainly stated that,

"And I will ask the Father, and he will give you another Advocate, who will never leave you. He is the Holy Spirit, who leads into all truth. The world cannot receive him, because it isn't looking for him and doesn't recognize him. But you know him, because he lives with you now and later will be in you. No, I will not abandon you as orphans—I will come to you."
John 14: 15-18 NLT

As we understand the purpose that the Holy Ghost was given, it is easy to see the parallel between what the Church was tasked to do, and what Adam was tasked to do.

"And God blessed them, and God said unto them, Be fruitful, and multiply, and replenish the earth, and subdue it: and have dominion over the fish of the sea, and over the fowl of the air, and over every living thing that moveth upon the earth." Genesis 1: 28

Then Jesus came to them and said,

"All authority in heaven and on earth has been given to me. Therefore go and make disciples of all nations, baptizing them in the name of the Father and of the Son and of the Holy Spirit, and teaching them to obey everything I have commanded you. And surely I am with you always, to the very end of the age." Matthew 28: 18-20 NIV

He said to them,

"Go into all the world and preach the gospel to all creation. Whoever believes and is baptized will be saved, but whoever does not believe will be condemned. And these signs will accompany those who believe: In my name they will drive out demons; they will speak in new tongues; they will pick up snakes with their hands, and when they drink deadly poison, it will not hurt them at all; they will place their hands on sick people, and they will get well." Mark 16: 15-18 NIV

When we look at these four scriptures, it should be obvious that both Adam and the body of apostles that Jesus left in charge of the 1st century New Testament Remnant Church were tasked

CHAPTER THREE: THE SUM TOTAL & THE REMNANT

with doing the same thing... reproduction. Both were commanded to replenish the earth with offspring after their own kind. They were commanded to populate the earth by multiplying, and reproducing themselves. Just as Adam and Eve were charged to be fruitful, the Church was commanded to do the same. If taking the Gospel message to the whole world is not a multiplication function, nothing else can be considered to be so. God authorized Adam to subdue the earth and have dominion over every living thing whether in the air, in the water, or in the earth. Surely that can be no greater than having dominion over demons, poison, and sickness. The extent of Adam's domain was increased to include the spiritual world also; as God charged the Church to fulfill her Adamic role.

The Church produces a resounding crescendo as she steps into her role as the designated representative and delegated authority for the God of creation. He has commissioned her to rule in His stead, until the "kingdoms of this world are offered up to the Kingdom of our God."[68] Just as Adam was chosen to be the steward over God's creation, so the Church has been chosen to be steward over the ministry Jesus has established in the earth. The Church is the caretaker of the gift of deliverance God has given to the inhabitants of the world. She is tasked to safeguard it better than Adam protected the domain he had been given charge of. Just as Adam was warned not to partake of the knowledge of evil, so the Church is charged to beware of the seducing doctrines of devils, designed to contaminate her, and cause her to fall from her position of power and influence.

The Church is the sum total and culmination of God's

intention to have a human vessel to stand guard over the provisions He has established for the sustenance of His creation, and the eternal relationship He seeks to have with His creation. The Father has intricately designed an agenda that allows man to exercise his gift of "free will," yet at the same time experience the benevolence of a loving father who has a stop gap in place to insure the salvation of His creation. The Church has the full authorization of Jehovah to perpetuate His divine intention of maintaining communion with the chosen subjects of His Kingdom. By employing the provisions of Covenant, which have been established to make sure that His subjects do in fact receive their rightful inheritance, the Church stands guard over God's most prized possession: His chosen people, the seed of Abraham. The Remnant Church is God's shining example of His amassed collection of all those seemingly disjointed parts, and His ability to cause them to be united, cohesive, and unified the sum total of His power, His wisdom, and His love. The remnant!

    The Remnant Church is the sum total of God's original intention for His redeemed creation after the Fall of Adam and Eve. After 'The Fall' of man, God didn't change His mind for man being His designated representative and delegated authority in the earth. The fact of the matter is that when God gathered Adam, Eve, and satan after the fruit was eaten, He could have ended that creation and started all over again. He did not rescind His command for man to multiply, be fruitful, and replenish the earth. He did not relieve man of his duty to subdue the earth and have dominion over it. Instead, He prophesied of the mechanism, the Messiah, that would crush the head of satan. He

CHAPTER THREE: THE SUM TOTAL & THE REMNANT

spoke into motion the provision He had put in place "from before the foundation of the world."⁶⁹ He still purposed for His creation to have fellowship with Him, and to still experience eternal life. He merely legislated that from now on, man's caretaking of the creation would be laborious, and woman's childbearing would be painful. Jehovah knew that after man abdicated his position of authority to satan, there would be a need for a vehicle to provide shetlter and empowerment to those emissaries who would still need to operate on His behalf. If God were to use man, after man fell from his place of innocence and authority, there had to be a way to restore man to the place he occupied before he fell. The Church represents God's way of restoration for His creation. She is the divine intervention necessary to thwart satan's plan to keep the creation separated from the Creator. The Church is God's way of placing mankind back in her rightful place of rulership over the earth. She is the unification of all the seemingly disconnected pieces from the results of the Fall, morphing into a creation demonstrating the outcome of God making Himself available to all who would receive Him. She is the sum total of Jehovah's worshippers empowered to continue Christ's ministry of reconciliation, through the power provided by the Holy Ghost on the Day of Pentecost. She is not an afterthought, but the zenith of an all-knowing God's plan to have a

> *"Just as Adam was warned not to partake of the knowledge of evil, so the Church is charged to beware of the seducing doctrines of devils, designed to contaminate her, and cause her to fall from her position of power and influence."*

people for Himself...the Church.

As we study the concept of the Remnant Church, we cannot do it without recognizing the intentions of God for Israel; relative to the concept of "the sum total." The Church is the sum total because she is the culmination of the "promise" God made to Abraham. In the precursor to the Old Covenant or Abrahamic Covenant, God promised Abraham that the whole earth would be blessed through the nation that came out of Abraham.[70] Abraham's seed produced the Hebrews, Israelites, known as the Jews. This was the ethnic group through which Jesus Christ came; Jesus was a practicing Jew. The Church is the inheritance of God. She is the fulfillment of His promise to Father Abraham; the culmination of the covenant He made with Abraham, Isaac, and Jacob. Another thing we must understand is that the Jews were not just given Canaan because they were so good. In fact, they disobeyed and disappointed God time and time again. The inhabitants of the land were so bad, that God decided to dispossess them, and use the Jewish nation as a light to point them towards the one true God. Although the Jews had a duty to rid the land of some of its wicked nations and their practices, they also had a duty to shed the light of the righteous worship of Jehovah. The Hebrews sinful ways prohibited them from fulfilling their duty and reaching the rest of their world for Jehovah. Jesus came to do what Israel failed to do; redeem the world.

As we define the concept of the Remnant Church, we must show a relationship between the general definition of "remnant" and the definition of the "Church." The remnant is the part of something that is left over when other parts are gone; it involves the notion of something smaller being used to accomplish that which the larger part failed to accomplish. The idea that something which is void of its other parts, parts which appeared to be necessary, is still able to function in the purpose and role for which it was created, and intended to be used is a mystery. The Church fits the definition of a remnant in many ways. She is the sum total of all of God's experiences with man since the Day of Pentecost. First of all, she is the part leftover when the overwhelming majority of earth's inhabitants refuse to accept Jesus Christ as their personal Savior, and consciously reject God's answer to the sin problem. She is the portion that remains acceptant of the idea of there being more than a higher power, but that there is rather a Creator, who is the One true and living God; Jehovah being His name. She is the remaining portion when the other parts of mankind are rushing down the wide path of destruction, towards a devil's hell. Hell is a place that is reserved for those who would rather serve their own self pleasures; as opposed to living a life surrendered to serving the Creator. The Church is a noticeably smaller group of people; they do not constitute a majority. Instead, she is much smaller numerically; yet she is so much stronger than the majority; due to the indwelling power of the God of creation; residing in her. Through the baptism of the Holy Ghost, being resident in the lives of her members, she has a supernatural advantage over the nonbelieving majority of humanity. While the larger majority is not able to submit itself

> *"The Remnant Church is the sum total of God's original intention for His redeemed creation after the Fall of Adam and Eve."*

to the Kingdom of God, this smaller portion gladly accepts the government of God in their lives, and positions themselves to carry on major spiritual warfare against the kingdom of darkness. She is able to accomplish what the majority cannot see themselves doing; embracing a God-centered life and a "selfless" agenda.

The fact that she is void of other gifts, graces and talents belonging to the majority does not impede her from functioning in her designated office; nor does it diminish her ability to fulfill her purpose. In spite of her small numerical size, she is still more than able to accomplish her God-given assignment. Although the Church is that portion which has been separated from the much larger mass of society, she is still capable of being the visible representation of the invisible God; in the earth today. She is still the conduit of His message of repentance, and a conductor of the power necessary to take a life off of the road to hell, and change it to a heavenly direction. She is able to help the "concept" of conversion become a life-changing "reality."

Yes, even though she is merely a remnant, merely a leftover, she is still able to embrace, fellowship, and help stabilize the uncountable number of those who are willing to receive the free gift of salvation through Jesus Christ our Lord. She IS the epitome, the apex, the pinnacle of all of the events that happened since the Fall of man, that have provided the opportunity for man to be ushered back into right relationship with God. The Remnant Church exists to help usher man back into his rightful position as God's designated representative and delegated authority in the earth.

While exploring the notion of The Remnant Church, it

CHAPTER THREE: THE SUM TOTAL & THE REMNANT

must be examined in conjunction with the after effects of the Jews who survived the initial Sanhedrin persecution; after the crucifixion and the Day of Pentecost. While the group who heard Peter's gospel message on the Day of Pentecost became the 1st century New Testament Remnant Church, we must recognize that a remnant also emerged out of that remnant. The 1st century Christians experienced a lot of persecution from the Sanhedrin, the Sadducees in particular. It is commonly believed, and held to be true, that the Sanhedrin was comprised of a mixture of Pharisees and Sadducees. The Sanhedrin was the supreme council, or court, in ancient Israel. The Sanhedrin was comprised of seventy men, plus the high priest, who served as its president. The members came from the chief priests, scribes and elders, but there is no record on how they were chosen. The Sanhedrin had its own police force which could arrest people, as they did Jesus Christ. While the Sanhedrin heard both civil and criminal cases, and could impose the death penalty, in New Testament times it did not have the authority to execute convicted criminals. That power was reserved for the Romans, which explains why Jesus was crucified—a Roman punishment— rather than stoned, according to Mosaic Law. The Sanhedrin were abolished after the Fall of Jerusalem in A.D. 70.[71]

Originally the Sanhedrin was an assembly of twenty to twenty-three men appointed in every city in the land of Israel. The Mishnah arrives at the number twenty-three based on an exegetical derivation. A "community" must be able to vote for both conviction and exoneration. The minimum size of a "community" is ten men, therefore, one more is required to achieve a majority. However, since a simple majority cannot convict, an additional judge is required. Finally, a court should not have an even number of judges to prevent deadlocks; thus twenty three. This court dealt with only religious matters. The court convened every day except festivals and Shabbat. The final binding decision of the Sanhedrin was in 358, when the Hebrew Calendar was adopted. Unfortunately, the Roman Empire dissolved the Sanhedrin during its persecution of the Jews. The Sanhedrin was an active participant in the trial of Jesus and the stoning death of Stephen. The Sanhedrin as a body claimed powers that lesser Jewish courts did not have. As such, they were the only ones who could try the king, extend the boundaries of the Temple and Jerusalem, and were the final authority on all questions of law. Before 191 B.C. the High Priest acted as the ex officio head of the Sanhedrin, but in 191 B.C., the Sanhedrin lost confidence in the High Priest.[72]

    The Sadducees were "sad, you see," because they did not believe in "resurrection from the dead," while the Pharisees did believe in resurrection. This might account as to why Nicodemeus sought to engage Jesus in a conversation about eternal life; Nicodemeus was a Pharisee. The Sadducees were a sect or group of Jews that were active in Judea during the Second Temple period, starting from the second century through the destruction of the Temple in 70 A.D. The sect was identified by Josephus with the upper social and economic echelon of Judean society. As a whole, the sect fulfilled various political, social, and religious roles, including maintaining the Temple. The Sadducees are often compared to other contemporaneous sects, including the Pharisees and the Essenes. Their sect is believed to have become extinct sometime after the destruction of Herod's Temple in Jerusalem in

70 A.D. The Sadducees rejected the Oral Law as proposed by the Pharisees. Rather, they saw the Torah as the sole source of divine authority. The written law, in its depiction of the priesthood, corroborated the power and enforced the authority of the Sadducees in Judean society. According to Josephus, the Sadducees believed that:

- There is no fate
- God does not commit evil
- Man has free will; "man has the free choice of good or evil"
- The soul is not immortal; there is no afterlife, and
- There are no rewards or penalties after death

The Sadducees rejected the belief in resurrection of the dead, which was a central tenet believed by Pharisees and by early Christians. The Sadducees supposedly believed in the traditional Jewish concept of Sheol for those who had died.[73]

Therefore, it should be easy to understand that in addition to the persecution of the 1st century Church being Sanhedrin driven, it probably originated with the Sadducees. The Sadducees were focused on stamping out "the Way," this brand of abhorrent Judaism that had the audacity to intentionally propagate the notion of a resurrection; with the promise of eternal life attached to it. They perceived the whole concept of Christianity or "the Way" as repugnant, repulsive, disgusting, and detestable. Is it any wonder that they so aggressively pursued the members of the 1st century Church, and vehemently put them to death? This same Sanhedrin had aggressively pursued Jesus, as He walked the sandy shores of Galilee. They were intent about stamping out His message, and had no reservation in delivering Him up to Herod for crucifixion. If they had been legally able, they would have stoned Jesus to death; according to the Law of Moses. Since the death penalty was beyond the Sanhedrin's scope of authority, Jesus ended up dying the Roman death of crucifixion. He who knew no sin became a curse for us; bringing to fruition what the Scriptures said about His death.[74]

The newly birthed 1st century Remnant Church was in the crosshairs of this anti-resurrection group of Jewish professionals, doctors, and clergy. They were seen as another unwanted sect that had separated itself from Orthodox Judaism. How dare they think that they could exercise a positional relationship with Jehovah that superseded the order which had been established by Father Abraham and the great prophet Moses? How dare Christ utter that He was greater than Abraham, and before Abraham was I AM! The Sanhedrin was appalled by the insolence of this poor prophet from Nazareth; because everyone knew that no prophet or good thing came out of Galilee.

"They answered and said unto him, Art thou also of Galilee? Search, and look: for out of Galilee ariseth no prophet." John 7:52

It is interesting to note that these Messianic Jews had become a small separated portion of a larger group. The large group had refused to believe that their Messiah would come as a lowly servant; instead of a reigning king. The two mainline prophecies concerning the Messiah depicted Him as a servant and a king. This small group became a remnant because they chose to

CHAPTER THREE: THE SUM TOTAL & THE REMNANT

believe that Messiah would first be a servant; then a king. That Messiah would, in fact, first be lowly, then exalted. This made sense. If the reverse were true, exalted then lowly; that would have been an embarrassment and a defeat. If it had not been in the purposes of God for the Jews to reject Jesus, in order to fulfill His prophecy concerning the seed of Abraham blessing the whole world to come to fruition, then even the Sanhedrin would have logically recognized that it made sense for the Messiah to come as a servant first. Maybe they would have accepted Jesus as their Messiah. Think about it, if you were looking for a savior, would you want him to come as a king first and then as a servant? That proposition makes no logical sense. So, from the start, this mixed remnant of Messianic Jews and converted Gentile proselytes were doomed to be the objects of massive persecution by the greatest Jewish minds of that day. They were doomed to be a casualty of the war between those who believed in the resurrection of the dead, and those who did not. Those who first dared to disassociate themselves with the synagogue, and become people of "the Way" were the targets of some of the worse self-inflicted genocide the world has ever seen. They were predestined to be a remnant.

Additionally, The Remnant Church must also be considered in terms of the aggregation of the saints who survived after 1st century Christianity was accepted by the Roman government, and subsequently the Church lost its apostolic flavor. There was a noticeable difference that happened to the Church when Rome accepted Christianity as the official religion of the empire. The group of Messianic Jews and proselytes which remained were survivors of a massive persecution leveled against them by the

Orthodox Jews and the Roman government. They were left over after the persecution that was leveled against that 1st century New Testament Remnant Church. They were those left over from the massive numbers that were added to the Church on the Day of Pentecost, and afterwards; who had not perished in the persecution. The remnant was now faced with another test of survival. They had to now position themselves to maintain the fervor, flavor, and virtue of that great group of called out ones; which had been established when Jesus, the Holy Ghost baptizer, returned and indwelt His original disciples and apostles.

This new remnant was now tasked with maintaining the power and authority that had been vested in the original 1st century New Testament Remnant Church. They were now in a situation where they had to maintain the apostolic flavor that had marked the apostles as those who had been with Christ. The same flavor that marked the disciples who had been with Jesus. The apostolic government that had been charged to oversee the ministry Christ left in the earth, after His ascension and return to dwell in the lives of believers, had just experienced a major coup. The enemy had just doused the Church with her first experience of compromise and conformity. The nature of membership in the body of believers called out from mainstream Judaism had experienced a drastic shift. No longer were the apostolic requirements of repentance and conversion in place, and mandatory. The requirements for membership had shifted.

Repentance deals with our thoughts, actions, motives, lifestyles, social customs, family and economic ties. There should not be a single area of our lives that is unaffected by our conscious turning from self-government to God-government. Repentance is a radical change that involves putting the axe to the root. As we separate ourselves from the nature of sin, we should allow the new God-consciousness to have free reign in every area of our lives. Repentance produces a conscious awareness of our rebellion to the law of God, and our basic sin nature; which is a spirit that is disconnected from God. It produces awareness that we are governing our own life, and not living a life subject to God's ways and rules. It allows us to see that we are moving in a direction that is opposite of God's direction, and in fact are moving away from Him; not towards Him.

The accompanying results of this awareness should result in us turning from our own self-will, and self-rule, to a place where we position ourselves under the Lordship of Jesus Christ. It should cause us to submit to the government of God in our lives, and allow the Spirit of God to convict us of sin, and convince us that we should be pursuing the ways of righteousness. Repentance is not optional. It is a command from God given to His people from their days of the kings, through the days of the prophets, through the days of the forerunner of the Christ, through the days of the Christ, through the days of the apostles, until NOW. It is God's call for man to forsake his ways, and change to the ways of God. Conversion expresses the action of the will, in turning to God. When we receive God's gift of repentance, we take the first step in the obedience of faith to be reconciled to God. Conversion involves the turning of a sinner to God. In a general sense the heathen are said to be "converted" when they abandon heathenism and embrace the Christian faith. In a more special sense, men are converted when, by the influence of divine grace in their souls, their whole life is changed, old things pass away, and all things become new.

> *"Repentance is a radical change that involves putting the axe to the root."*

The Biblical root of the word conversion conveys the idea of turning. To turn to embrace God, or to turn to Judaism from a Gentile lifestyle. It usually follows repentance, requires self-examination, and is accomplished by faith and the power of The Holy Spirit. It is commanded, necessary, and is accompanied by confession of sin and prayer. These scriptural requirements of repentance and conversion had disappeared. No longer was there a need to have the evidence of a changed lifestyle; as a requisite for membership. No longer was there a need for a sacrificial shift in priorities, and no longer an urgent need to share the "faith" with those who were not a part of "the Way." No longer was there an urgency to demonstrate a commitment to carry out "The Great Commission." The requirements for membership had shifted.

The lines in the sand had shifted, the battle plan had been watered down, and purity of the relationship with Jehovah had been compromised. After the persecution ended, tolerance became normal, and the sense of uniqueness also dissipated. No longer were there stringent requirements necessary to be identified with "the Church;" but now, a more relaxed atmosphere existed. You no longer had to change your ways, and entry into the Church was as easy as being sprinkled with water; not immersed and buried in a watery grave. Or you could be simply physically born into the

Church; if your parents were members of the church. No longer did you have to be spiritually reborn; the physical elements of entry were deemed to be adequate to consider yourself a part of the church. If the truth be told, these requirements were enough to be a part of the physical church that the Roman Empire had crafted. However, they were sorely inadequate to be a part of the Universal Church; the Body of Christ.

It is of paramount importance to maintain the distinction between these two bodies as we examine the history of the Church from that point onward. Although we do recognize that the first fifteen centuries of Christianity took place under the structural churches that were created by the Western Roman Catholic Church and the Eastern Orthodox Church, we must never fail to remember that the basis and original belief systems of those organizations drastically differed from the apostolic traditions and practices upon which the 1st century New Testament Remnant Church was founded. As we have stated previously, we will attempt to reiterate again. When the governance of the New Testament Church was wrestled out of the hands of her Jewish apostolic overseers, and placed into the hands of political appointees of the Roman Empire; she began her journey down the road to her dark ages. The 1st century New Testament Remnant Church did not begin to experience her restoration until the Protestant Reformation of 1512.

When Rome took over the governance of Christianity, yet another remnant emerged. Even though some pagan practices were introduced into the religious body known as Christians, there were still bodies of Messianic Jews and Christians, who had been proselytes of Judaism, who still continued the worship practices that had been instituted by those original believers who were immersed in the apostle's doctrine.[75] There was yet a remnant who maintained the ways of the original body of believers that had been formed on the Day of Pentecost, and other times close to that event. There was still a residue of those who adhered to the tenets of faith upon which this great Christianity was built. There always was, has been, and always will be a remnant.

As we look at The Remnant Church, it is impossible to substantiate the need for her existence without evaluating the impact the saints who survived after the Protestant Reformation had. What effect did they have on the emergence of a new way of relating to Jehovah; God of the Hebrews? We must also examine the impact the subsequent rescue of the Church from Rome and Catholicism, had on the Body of Christ. We must remember that for fifteen centuries, the majority of those who practiced Christianity did so under the auspices of the Western Roman Catholic Church and the Eastern Orthodox Church. All that the world knew of the religion that was formed, when some practitioners of Judaism decided to follow the prophet from Nazareth, was manifested in the morphing of those original remnant-based belief systems with what was birthed in Rome, Alexandria, and Constantinople. Christianity no longer resembled what we read of in the book of Acts, but it now had a new look and flavor. It was compromised with an infusion of practices associated with the "worship of the sun." Although Rome had embraced some of the basic tenets of the Christian faith, she had still held on to some of her own major pagan practices.

Rome had subtly blended those pagan practices into the basic Jewish tenets and worship forms of the Judeo Christian faith. As we chronicle the growth of Christianity in a pagan world, which was widely acceptant of the worship of false gods, gods other than Jehovah, the God of the Hebrews, there is a stark reality we must face. The non-Christian nations were seeing a worship form that had lost its initial Jewish flavor. They were seeing a compromised form, which in many instances paralleled, and resembled, their own worship form. They saw the inclusion of statues, which resembled their own way of representing their idols, graven images of their gods. Is it any wonder that it was so easy to evangelize the world with this pre-Protestant Reformation brand of Christianity.

Many major cultures had their own version of the Virgin Mary and the baby Jesus. For an in-depth reading on the subject, I recommend, "The Two Babylons," by Hislop.[76] It is important to note that there was a major deviation from the apostle's doctrine, upon which the Church had been founded, and more of an inclusion of some of the ways of the "sun worshippers." This was done to make those being recruited feel comfortable with their forced acceptance of Christianity. We must acknowledge that the church that resulted from the inclusion of government into religion, that hybrid, was not necessarily full of the pure virtue of the New Testament Remnant Church from which it had originated. There were deceptive ways and compromises, which were interjected into the original belief system, that resulted in a weakened form of an otherwise acknowledged extreme way of life. The inclusion of government oversight and pagan practices, into the New Testament Remnant Church, diminished the effectiveness of Christianity to produce lifechanging behavior in the lives of her practitioners. Therefore, it was necessary for a remnant to arise to rescue the organism which had started as the 1st century New Testament Remnant Church. She had evolved into the Western Roman Catholic and Eastern Orthodox Churches, and needed to be saved.

Therefore, a condition existed for emergence of a body that would maintain the original values of the Church. There was a need for her to come forth out of those compromised organizations, and properly represent the intentions and design of the Father; when He mandated the Son to form the "ecclesia." As a result, another Remnant Church arrived on the scene; the Pre-Protestant Reformation Remnant Church. She was mandated to fulfill the prophetic destiny of the 1st century New Testament Remnant Church, and become the culmination of what was formed as the apostles and disciples followed the Master's command. She was to represent the end-result as they obeyed to move forth to disciple the nations. Worldly deception had crept into the New Testament Church. God had to separate a portion that still had the residue of the Day of Pentecost noticeably present in its spiritual DNA, because of the compromise that tainted the holiness of that 1st century remnant group. There had to be a remnant that could shake off the effects of the infiltration of the Roman Empire into Christianity. Hence the pre-Protestant Reformation remnant was birthed. Long before the official Protestant Reformation, there was a group of devout Roman Catholics that were crying, "Holy, Holy, Holy; Lord God Almighty; early in the morning our song shall rise to Thee."

CHAPTER THREE: THE SUM TOTAL & THE REMNANT

Just as there was a group of devout, God-fearing Jews who recognized the advent of Messiah in the earth; a Roman Catholic remnant emerged. Just as when a group of devout God fearing Jews and proselytes who heard the 'sound' that came as a result of the mighty rushing wind from heaven filling the room where the apostles and disciples were gathered and praying in one accord; a Roman Catholic remnant emerged. Even as this group of God fearing Roman Catholic Christians who recognized the error of incorporating the practices of "sun worshippers" into the liturgy of those who celebrated Jesus of Nazareth as God's messiah to the world; a remnant emerged. Even so, after these Roman Catholics protested and began to reform the way Christianity was practiced, and God began to restore moves of the Spirit back into the Body of Christ, and even unto this day a remnant was and is emerging.

As the Church was being positioned to move back to her place of origin, in as much as holiness and a changed lifestyle is concerned, a remnant was emerging out of each restorative movement she experienced. Jehovah has continually been perfecting the Church, as she moves towards the end of the age. Her perfection or maturity is going to be necessary in order for her to seamlessly assimilate into the invading Army of Heaven. In order for there to be no glitches, or gaps in performance in the Army of God, a remnant had to arise out of each move of God in the Church. This was necessary so that the integrity of the 1st century New Testament Remnant Church could be maintained, and the essence of what she was intended to be could be ensured. Too often, the Body of Christ becomes so attached to the move of the Spirit that the Church has just experienced, that she fails to see the big picture, and just how that move contributes to the total on-going purpose of God for the Church. Invariably, we sometimes will see a whole niche, or worship form, created by a move of God as the be all and end all of the move of God. When in actuality, that move was really intended to only be a part of the total continual perfecting of the Church. In all truthfulness, the move was only intended to be the creation of a springboard for a whole new movement to further advance the purposes of God; as He moves the Church to maturity.

> *"Jehovah has continually been perfecting the Church, as she moves towards the end of the age."*

After the surge that resulted from the Reformation, the Church began to settle into the normalcy of being comfortable with the restorative power of God. As He moved the Church back to her rightful place of prominence, there yet arose another need for a Remnant Church. There had to be a people who were more preoccupied with having a meaningful and intimate relationship with Jehovah, and not as preoccupied with the restorative moves of God they were seeing. We have seen it over and over again; with movements as basic as speaking in tongues, to movements as bizarre as handling snakes, roaring like a lion, holy laughter, and rolling on the floor. While God may have intended these to be a part of the move of the Spirit in the Church, He certainly did not intend for us to get stuck "there," and not move on to perfection. While those movements may have been beneficial for the Body of Christ, they were only designed to be a pit stop; not her final destination. Here again, it became necessary for God to extract a

CHAPTER THREE: THE SUM TOTAL & THE REMNANT

portion from the benefactors of those movements that He could depend on to stay faithful and focused. There had to be those who were dedicated to the attainment of the measure of the stature of the fullness of Christ. The same measure that was found in the 1st century New Testament Remnant Church is the same measure that Jehovah is trying to develop in the Church; even to this time. As He extracted remnants out of those movements, He was and is purposefully moving the Church to her final destination, the End Times Remnant Church.

With all of the false doctrine being perpetrated in, or on, the Church by the god of this world, there was definitely a need for those saints who survived the carnage, and rose from the aftermath of the satanic attack, to reformulate their relationship to and worship of the God of creation. As God continued to drive the Church back to her original form and intensity; the mode in which she operated at her inception, the enemy's attack persisted. The god of this world operates by deception. He entices man to compromise his stance, in order for man to experience self-satisfaction. These were the methods he attempted to use on Jesus, when he tempted Him for those forty days and nights in the wilderness. The lust of the flesh, the lust of the eyes, and the pride of life are exactly what he used then, and now uses to try to prevent the Church from reaching her ultimate destination. As is his way, the enemy doesn't just use an outright lie that would insult the Church's spiritual intelligence. Instead, he slightly distorts the truth, in an attempt to deceive her into accepting his half-truth. Therefore, he preys on folks who are not rooted and grounded in the Word of God. He is always searching for those who are content to allow those in church leadership to tell them what God is saying, as opposed to studying His Word, and seeking the face, and heart of God for themselves.

It is incumbent upon every saint of God to STUDY the Bible, in order to understand exactly what the will and purposes of God are. Every believer has to spend quality time with the Scriptures, in order not to be duped by the half-truths of satan. It is not enough just to read the Bible; it must be studied and cross-referenced; line upon line, precept upon precept. As the Church studies the Word of God, she must do it from the perspective of understanding who wrote the Scriptures, and the audience to whom those words were written. If the Church is ever to truly understand her place in the plan of God, and in relationship to the fulfillment of apocalyptic prophecy, she must understand the Scriptures through the Jewish filter in which they were written. Failure on her part to do so, will result in the body of Christ missing the timing of God, misappropriating ministry resources, failing to fulfill her purpose, and a total lack of accomplishing her God-ordained destiny.

The sad tragedy is that there have been countless deceptions aimed at the Church. They have been perpetrated by the enemy, and have been designed to de-intensify the energy with which the Church focuses her warfare against the kingdom of darkness, and commits to its destruction. Again, we must note that these have appeared in the form of subtle, understated, elusive propositions; as opposed to blatant outright lies. The enemy's goal is to devalue the concepts of holiness and righteousness. Some of the main deceptive doctrines which have slipped into the Church

CHAPTER THREE: THE SUM TOTAL & THE REMNANT

include: moderate drinking; acceptance of homosexuality as an alternate lifestyle; tolerance of tobacco usage; relaxed sexual standards; immodest dressing; salvation without repentance; hell as a condition only on earth alone, not a spiritual reality, not an after death experience; seven year tribulation period; pretribulation rapture; acceptance of games of chance; no need for the baptism of The Holy Spirit; acceptance of worldly music as a part of worship; sensual dancing; line dancing; no need for water baptism; membership vs. relationship, and replacement theology. All of the aforementioned things serve to undermine the authority of The Holy Spirit to govern our lives in a manner which demonstrates our obedience to the mandate to accurately characterize our existence. We are Jehovah's delegated authority and designated representatives in the earth. We must reflect His character.

> *"It is incumbent upon every saint of God to STUDY the Bible, in order to understand exactly what the will and purposes of God are."*

In addition to this, these things directly impact the nature of our spiritual warfare, and the sense of urgency with which we attempt to demobilize, and incapacitate, the kingdom of darkness. There is a gigantic list of organizations and religious entities that have been associated with the term "cult." Rather than engage in an exhaustive accusatory process of naming them, we will refer you to a couple of works you can explore, and allow the Spirit of God to speak to you. We will, however, name some of the deceptive practices of these groups. Here is a list of books you should explore:

"Handbook of Today's Religions" Josh McDowell and Don Stewart, *Here's Life Publishers, Inc*

"New Age Cults & Religions Texe Marrs", *Living Truth Publisher*

"Handbook of Denominations in the United States, *Abingdon Press*

"The Hidden Danger of the Rainbow" Constance Cumbey, *Huntington House Inc.*

"Unmasking the Jezebel Spirit" John Paul Jackson, *Stream Publications*

"Cheque Mate – The Game of Princes" Jeffrey A. Baker, *Whitaker House*

These works will give you insight into the groups and deceptive philosophies against which the remnant must be on guard. There are some extremely dangerous practices that have infiltrated the Church, in the name of Christianity. Some of these practices are not only anti-Christ, but are occultist in nature and origin. These doctrines embrace fundamental practices which are designed to appeal to man's basic human need to be loved, feel needed, and sense that our lives have meaning and direction. They usually center on new interpretation of the Holy Scriptures; with the underlying notion being that they alone have the key to interpreting the Scriptures correctly. Their interpretation is usually drastically different from the tenets of orthodox Christianity, and serves to support their organizational beliefs. These organizational beliefs are also usually drastically different from those espoused by orthodox, mainstream Christianity. In addition to sometimes having sources of authority which are non-Biblical in nature, these doctrines also have been known to: reject orthodox Christianity;

propagate a non-Biblical teaching denying the nature of God being a triune deity; believe in salvation by works; be characterized by the interpretive teachings of a strong founder; engage in false prophecy concerning the second coming of Christ, and have a theology that is ever changing, and constantly evolving.

We are not talking about the doctrines which have out right denied that Jesus was the Son of God, and merely relegated Him to being just another prophet. We are speaking of the deceptions that teach that Jesus Christ is not God in human flesh, but merely another created being. They deny the deity of Christ, stating that while He was a god; He was not Almighty God. They have revived the ancient heresy known as Arianism. These heresies also teach that Jesus Christ was a "preexistent spirit," and not the "unique Son of God;" but merely a preexistent spirit like the rest of us. These deceptive teachings also assert that The Holy Spirit is not a part of the Godhead, and is not God. They do not believe in the doctrine of the triune God (Trinity). Please note that these teachings are not relegated to one individual group, but are believed by many "supposedly" Christian organizations. These heresies also reject the notion of salvation being a free gift received by faith, but rather see it as an object to be earned by works. Furthermore, they do not believe that mankind needs to be saved from the inherent "sin nature" that was passed onto mankind due to the "original sin" of our father, Adam. While yet others state that there is "no need,

> "Jehovah has continually been perfecting the Church, as she moves towards the end of the age."

or requirement" for salvation or repentance; all of these are being passed off as Christian doctrines.

They also do not subscribe to the existence of a burning hell; an everlasting place of punishment and torment. The denial of this Biblical fact removes the fear of not obeying the commands of God, and removes any consequences for not receiving Jesus Christ as one's Savior and Lord. Many of these seducing doctrines do not recognize the canonized version of the Holy Bible as the inerrant, indisputable Word of God. They contend that it is incomplete, and that it is merely the works of mortal man; as opposed to The Holy Spirit inspired Word of God, penned by mortal men. This heresy gives reason to doubt the words found within the pages of the Holy Bible; thereby undermining and questioning the veracity, authenticity, and authority of the Bible. Since faith is the unquestioning trust and confidence in the Word we have heard from God, this doctrine has the potential to weaken our faith. All of this is to say nothing for the hundreds of supposedly Christian organizations that have been established where the Bible is not the final source of authority and more credence is given to the organizations publications; or the writings of their founder.

An untold number of organizations with belief systems originating in the occult have seeped into Christian churches. Secret organizations and societies, that secretly are immersed in luciferian worship, have been allowed to practice their rites inside of Church buildings, and hold offices; even the office of Pastor. God have mercy on the Church, for she has allowed a host of occult practices to penetrate her gates. Practices such as: fortune telling, hypnotism, magic shows, tea leaf reading, horoscope parties, card parties, séances, Harry Potter books and movies, are as common as Bible study, choir rehearsal, and Sunday school. All of these practices are happening within the walls of some local assemblies.

> *"An untold number of organizations with belief systems originating in the occult have seeped into Christian churches."*

In addition to some of the common cult practices that have been allowed to flourish under the banner of Christianity, there has been a frightening explosion of New Age religions within the corridors of our Christian society. The ranks of the New Age are growing exponentially, and they are even promoting themselves now as "The New Age Religion." There is a preponderance of organizations from Adelphi to the Worldwide Church of God; that are steeped in the New Age philosophy of worshipping whatever god, or higher power, you choose. Groups like Christian Science, Church of Divine Man, Life Spring, Transcendental Meditation, Unity Church, and a vast number of others are permitted to peacefully coexist within the context of our Judeo-Christian democracy.

It is the scathing searing of these doctrines and heresies that the End Times Remnant Church must be careful of, and guarded against. She cannot allow her principles and standards to be polluted by these seductive, compromising dogmas. The remnant must rise above the fray, and not permit her standards of holiness, and consecration to Jehovah, to be tainted by all of these deceptive doctrines of devils; that the enemy is hurling at the Church. The set of guidelines established by Jesus and the apostles, must be the same set of guidelines in operation as Messiah Jesus returns for His bride; the Church. The End Times Remnant Church must mirror the virtue of the 1st century New Testament Remnant Church, to be identifiable as the Church the Lord is looking for, as He returns trying to find "faithfulness." Let the remnant arise! The Remnant Church is intended to be the sum total of all things that God is, to operate in the power and holiness that He deems necessary to attract non-believing Israel and Gentiles, and to wage war against the kingdom of darkness. She must guard herself against the deceptive doctrines the enemy tries to use to inject compromise and conformity into the essence of who the Church really is.

CHAPTER THREE: THE SUM TOTAL & THE REMNANT

Please look forward to the "Remnant Church" volume 2

Endnotes

Chapter One

1 Edict of Toleration 311 A.D., Edict of Milan 313 A.D.
2 Revelation 12:9
3 Revelation 13:4, 7, 12-15; Revelation 19:20; Revelation 20:7-10
4 II Peter 2:1-2; II Timothy 4:3-4
5 II Kings 25:11; Jeremiah 37:13-14; Joshua 22:22; II Chronicles 29:19; II Chronicles 33:19; Jeremiah 2:19, 8:5
6 Acts 21:21; II Thessalonians 2:3
7 "Holman Bible Dictionary"; Holman Bible Publishers; Nashville, TN
8 Jeremiah 23:1-3; II Kings. 21:11-15
9 Genesis 7:11-22
10 Genesis 19:29-30
11 Genesis 45:1-46
12 Genesis 15:7-1
13 I Kings. 18:10-20
14 Daniel 6:7-23
15 Daniel 3:1-30
16 Judges 7:1-25
17 Isaiah 7:3
18 Jeremiah 23:3; Ezekiel 14:22; Amos 5:15; Micah 5:7; Zechariah 8:12

Chapter Two

19 John 1:11-12
20 Ephesians 2:20-22
21 The Crusaders, Volume 11; published by Chick Publications, Chino CA; "Sabotage", Page 19

22   "Constantine" by Ramsay Mac Mullen; published by the Dial Press; Crosscurrents in World History Series, New York, 1969, Page 72

23   "The Eternal Church" references; notes page 2; by Dr. Bill Hamon; Destiny Image Publishers; Inc., Shippensburg, PA

24   "The Eternal Church"; pg. 94-95; by Dr. Bill Hamon; Destiny Image Publishers, Inc.; Shippensburg, PA

25   "Church History", Vol. 1; Newman

26   "Which Bible?" by David Otis Fuller, D.D., Institute for Biblical Textual Studies, 2233 Michigan Street, NE, Grand Rapids, MI 49503; "God Only Wrote One Bible" by J. J. Ray, The Eye Opener Publishers, P.O. Box 7944, Eugene, OR 97401; "Manuscript Evidence" by P. S. Ruckman, Bible Baptist Bookstore, P.O. Box 7135, Pensacola, FL 32534; "The King James Version Defended" by Edward F. Hills, Th.D., Order from the Eye Opener Publishers, P.O. Box 7944, Eugene, OR 97401

27   "Constantine" published by Ramsay Mac Mullen; Page 112

28   The Crusaders, Volume 11, published by J.T.C., Chino CA, "Sabotage", Page 23

29   "The Two Babylons" by Hislop; published by Loizeaux Bros.; Neptune, NJ; chapter entitled 'The Mother of the Child

30   Romans 9th, 10th, & 11th chapters

31   Isaiah 10:20-27

32   Romans 11:25-27

33   Romans 11:26-32

34   Romans 9:22-27

35   Romans 11:11-24

36   Romans 11:25-27

37   Matthew 24:11-14; II Timothy 4:1-4; II Thessalonians 2:3; I

Timothy 4:1

38	Genesis 16:1-16
39	Genesis 21:9-21
40	Ephesians 2:11-22
41	Galatians 3:26-29
42	Genesis 1:27-28
43	Hebrews 9:22; Lev. 17:11
44	Galatians 3:26-29
45	Matthew 10:34-39; Luke 12:51
46	Haggai 2:7-9
47	Romans 1:16; Acts 13:44-48
48	Luke 3:23-38
49	Genesis 5: 1-32
50	Exodus 12:29-36
51	Genesis 41:25-41
52	Exodus 12:37-42
53	Exodus 12:24-28
54	I Kings. 11:1-10
55	I Kings. 11:29-40
56	Hebrews 7:11-17
57	Joel 2:17-27
58	Romans 11:4-5; Romans 11:25-26
59	Leviticus 10:1; Numbers 26:61
60	John 20:19-23
61	Acts 1:1-8, 15-16; Acts 2:1-4
62	Acts 2:9-11
63	Wikipedia – The Free Encyclopedia
64	Wikipedia – The Free Encyclopedia
65	Theopedia – An Encyclopedia of Biblical Christianity

66   Theopedia – An Encyclopedia of Biblical Christianity
67   Theopedia – An Encyclopedia of Biblical Christianity

Chapter Three
68   Revelation 11:15
69   Ephesians 1:4; Revelation 13:8
70   Genesis 12:1-3
71   www.About.com; Christianity; Jack Zavada
72   Wikipedia – The Free Encyclopedia
73   Wikipedia – The Free Encyclopedia
74   Isaiah 53:12; Mark 15:27-28; Galatians 3:13; Deuteronomy. 21:23
75   Wikipedia – The Free Encyclopedia
76   "The Two Babylons" by Hislop; published by Loizeaux Bros., Neptune, NJ

www.ingramcontent.com/pod-product-compliance
Lightning Source LLC
Chambersburg PA
CBHW072018110526
44592CB00012B/1362